International Research in Healthcare

Felicity Smith
BPharm (hons), MA, PhD, MRPharmS
Professor of Pharmacy Practice
School of Pharmacy, University of London, UK

Sally-Anne Francis
BPharm (hons), PhD, MRPharmS
Honorary Senior Lecturer
School of Pharmacy, University of London, UK

Ellen Schafheutle
MSc, MRes, PhD, MRPharmS
Research Fellow
School of Pharmacy and Pharmaceutical Sciences
University of Manchester, UK

London • Chicago **Pharmaceutical Press**

Published by the Pharmaceutical Press
An imprint of RPS Publishing

1 Lambeth High Street, London SE1 7JN, UK
100 South Atkinson Road, Suite 200, Grayslake, IL 60030-7820, USA

© Pharmaceutical Press 2008

(**PₕP**) is a trade mark of RPS Publishing

RPS Publishing is the publishing organisation of the
Royal Pharmaceutical Society of Great Britain

First published 2008

Typeset by Type Study, Scarborough, North Yorkshire
Printed in Great Britain by TJ International, Padstow, Cornwall

ISBN 978 0 85369 750 3

Contents

International Research in Healthcare

ULLA Pharmacy series

Series Editors-in-Chief

Professor Alexander T Florence
CBE, DSc, FRSC, FRSE, FRPharmS
The School of Pharmacy, University of London, UK

Professor Anthony C Moffat
BPharm, PhD, DSc, CChem, FRSC, FRPharmS
The School of Pharmacy, University of London, UK

Members of the Editorial Advisory Board

Professor Eva Brittebo, Uppsala University, Faculty of Pharmacy, Uppsala, Sweden

Professor Lennart Dencker, Uppsala University, Faculty of Pharmacy, Uppsala, Sweden

Professor Sven Frokjaer, University of Copenhagen, Faculty of Pharmaceutical Sciences, Copenhagen, Denmark

Professor Denis Labarre, University Paris South, Faculty of Pharmacy, Paris, France

Professor Ulf Madsen, University of Copenhagen, Faculty of Pharmaceutical Sciences, Copenhagen, Denmark

Professor Gerard J Mulder, Leiden/Amsterdam Centre for Drug Research, Free University, Leiden, The Netherlands

Professor Anne-Marie Quéro, University Paris South, Faculty of Pharmacy, Paris, France

Professor Henk Timmerman, Leiden/Amsterdam Centre for Drug Research, Department of Medicinal Chemistry, Amsterdam, The Netherlands

Other titles in the ULLA pharmacy series include:
Pharmaceutical Toxicology
Paediatric Drug Handling
Molecular Biopharmaceutics
Proteomics and Metabolomics in Pharmaceutical Science
Biomedical and Pharmaceutical Polymers

NB: some of titles listed are forthcoming/not yet published

ULLA pharmacy series

Series Editors-in-Chief

Professor Alexander T Florence and **Professor Anthony C Moffat**, The School of Pharmacy, University of London, UK

The ULLA series is a new and innovative series of introductory textbooks for students of pharmacy and pharmaceutical sciences.

This new series is produced by the ULLA Consortium (European University Consortium for Advanced Pharmaceutical Education and Research). The Consortium is a European academic collaboration in research and teaching of the pharmaceutical sciences that is constantly growing and expanding. The Consortium was founded in 1992 and consists of departments of pharmacy and pharmaceutical sciences from leading universities throughout Europe:

- Faculty of Pharmacy, University of Uppsala, Sweden
- The School of Pharmacy, University of London, UK
- Leiden/Amsterdam Centre for Drug Research, University of Leiden, The Netherlands
- Leiden/Amsterdam Centre for Drug Research, Free University, Amsterdam, The Netherlands
- University of Copenhagen, Faculty of Pharmaceutical Sciences, Copenhagen, Denmark
- Faculty of Pharmacy, University Paris South, France
- Faculty of Pharmacy, University of Parma, Italy.

The editorial board for the ULLA series consists of several academics from these leading European Institutions who are all experts in their individual field of pharmaceutical science.

The titles in this new groundbreaking series are primarily aimed at European PhD students and will also have global appeal to postgraduate students undertaking masters or diploma courses, undergraduates for specific courses and practising pharmaceutical scientists.

Further information on the Consortium can be found at www.u-l-l-a.org.

Preface

This text is intended for researchers in health services, medicines use and professional practice who are undertaking a multi-centre research project involving data collection in, or relating to, more than one country. Research across international boundaries presents its own challenges in that attention has to be paid to the relevance of research objectives, and feasibility of procedures in different settings while maintaining a scientific approach in terms of design, instruments and execution.

The book is designed to provide guidance for researchers in the preparation, planning, management and execution of their work, taking into account the impact of differing political, organisational, social and cultural contexts that international work presents. It is organised into chapters which, in a logical order, focus on each stage of the research process from preparatory work and setting up the project to analysis and dissemination of results. Each chapter outlines theoretical principles that should be observed in any project, highlighting and addressing the particular challenges of their application in an international context. The book also draws on the experiences of researchers who have undertaken international projects to illustrate approaches to ensuring, for example, the relevance of objectives, comparability of data and acceptability of research procedures in different countries and settings. While the text was originally conceived with researchers in pharmacy and related disciplines in mind, which is reflected in the affiliations of contributors, the text will be equally relevant to health service researchers from a range of disciplines, backgrounds and other health professions.

How this text will differ from competing texts

Throughout the world the roles of the health professions in the provision and delivery of healthcare is continually being appraised and evaluated in the light of local public health priorities. Health professionals worldwide are continually striving to develop services that are responsive to local needs, sensitive to circumstances and perspectives within communities, while contributing to wider (often national) health policy objectives. Across international boundaries there are many common themes, problems and policy objectives regarding healthcare, pharmaceutical policy, the use of medicines and the place of health professionals. At the same time, each country is unique in terms of its healthcare needs, patterns of provision of care, socio-cultural contexts that determine its uptake and consequently its research priorities. Similarly, in many countries research into healthcare, medicines use and professional practice is well established, while in others this is less so.

Many previous texts have been dedicated to research methods that are employed to investigate and evaluate health services and the use of medicines. This book differs from existing texts in that it specifically addresses the challenges to researchers of undertaking studies across international boundaries to ensure that they are successfully executed, scientific in approach and valuable in terms of their findings.

Felicity Smith, Sally-Anne Francis and
Ellen Schafheutle
April 2008

About the authors

Felicity Smith is Professor of Pharmacy Practice at the School of Pharmacy, University of London. She has 20 years' experience of active involvement in research focusing on the use of medicines, health services and pharmacy practice. She has expertise in the application of a wide range of health services research methodologies and had responsibility for, and participated in, many multi-centre and international collaborations.

Sally-Anne Francis is Honorary Senior Lecturer at the School of Pharmacy, University of London, having previously held the appointments of lecturer and senior lecturer. She has worked closely with pharmacists from many countries through her directorship of a Master's programme in Clinical Pharmacy, International Practice and Policy. As an active health services researcher throughout the last 15 years, the focus of her research programme has been the relationship between drug therapy and quality of life of vulnerable populations, including the development of relevant health services that acknowledge patients' preferences and reduce the risks associated with medicines.

Ellen Schafheutle is Research Fellow at the School of Pharmacy & Pharmaceutical Sciences at the University of Manchester. Following her undergraduate pharmacy training in Germany, Ellen moved to Manchester in 1993, where she has been actively involved in research into the use of, and access, to medicines, and influences on professional practice. She has knowledge and experience in the use of a wide range of health services research methodologies, has worked on teams with multidisciplinary backgrounds and has been involved in a European collaboration.

List of contributors

Anna Birna Almarsdóttir
Professor, Faculty of Pharmacy, University of Iceland, Iceland

Claire Anderson
Professor of Social Pharmacy, School of Pharmacy, The University of Nottingham, UK

Ian Bates
Professor and Head of Educational Development, The School of Pharmacy, University of London, UK

Kerstin (Chris) Bingefors
Senior Lecturer, Pharmacoepidemiology and Pharmacoeconomics, Department of Pharmacy, Uppsala University, Uppsala, Sweden

Tina Brock
Senior Manager, Management Sciences for Health, Arlington, VA, USA

Filipa A Costa
Senior Lecturer, Instituto Superior de Ciências da Saúde Egas Moniz (ISCSEM), Portugal

Dana Darwish
Former PhD Student, The School of Pharmacy, University of London, UK

Bryony Dean Franklin
Director, Centre for Medication Safety and Service Policy, Hammersmith Hospitals NHS Trust and School of Pharmacy, University of London, UK

Catherine Duggan
Senior Clinical Lecturer, The School of Pharmacy, University of London, UK

Nicola Gray
Lecturer in Pharmacy Practice, School of Pharmacy, The University of Nottingham, UK

Mara Pereira Guerreiro
PhD student, School of Pharmacy & Pharmaceutical Sciences, The University of Manchester, UK

Karen Hassell
Professor of Social Pharmacy, School of Pharmacy & Pharmaceutical Sciences, The University of Manchester, UK

Michael Heinrich
Head of Centre and Professor, Centre for Pharmacognosy and Phyto-therapy, School of Pharmacy, University of London, UK

Carmel Hughes
Professor of Primary Care Pharmacy, School of Pharmacy, Queen's University, Belfast, Northern Ireland

Chuenjid Kongkaew
PhD Student, School of Pharmacy & Pharmaceutical Sciences, The University of Manchester, UK

James C McElnay
Professor of Pharmacy Practice, Clinical and Practice Research Group, School of Pharmacy, Queen's University, Belfast, Northern Ireland

Sabine Nebel
Former member of LFN Consortium, The School of Pharmacy, University of London, UK

Frances Owusu-Daaku
Senior Lecturer and Head, Department of Clinical and Social Pharmacy, Kwame Nkrumah University of Science and Technology, Kumasi, Ghana

Marion Schaeffer
Professor of Pharmacoepidemiology, Charité University Medicine, Humboldt-Universität, Berlin, Germany

Ellen Schafheutle
Research Fellow, School of Pharmacy & Pharmaceutical Sciences, The University of Manchester, UK

Felicity Smith
Professor of Pharmacy Practice, The School of Pharmacy, University of London, UK

David Taylor
Professor, The School of Pharmacy, University of London, UK

Janine Traulsen
Associate Professor, Copenhagen University, Denmark

Mary Tully
Clinical Senior Lecturer, School of Pharmacy & Pharmaceutical Sciences, The University of Manchester, UK

Tana Wuliji
Project Coordinator, International Pharmaceutical Federation, School of Pharmacy, University of London, UK

List of personal accounts

1

International perspectives on healthcare, medicines use and professional practice

The purpose of this introductory chapter is to set the scene for this book. It will outline some of the important international priorities with respect to health, healthcare, pharmaceutical policy, use of medicines and the place of health professionals. To be most effectively tackled, many of these issues need to be conceptualised and addressed in an international context which may be regional or include more diverse partners. The interdependence between nations, the need for co-operative and concerted actions to achieve mutually beneficial goals is widely recognised. While international studies will inevitably present additional challenges over and above local or national studies, there is an increasing appreciation of the value of international collaboration in research.

Global health agendas: the use of medicines and place of pharmacy

Issues around healthcare services, public health priorities and the provision and use of pharmaceuticals are high on international policy agenda. Prominent among these are the following:

- Ageing populations and rising costs of healthcare
- The advent of new, expensive therapies
- Worldwide increases in morbidity and mortality from chronic disease
- Global shortages in the health workforce, in particular imbalances between countries and differential impact of migration of health professionals
- The prevalence of counterfeit products
- Well-documented problems of irrational use of medicines, especially in less developed countries
- International commitment to the Millennium Development Goals

- Supply of, and equitable access to, medicines
- Availability and access to medicines for infectious disease
- Social and cultural contexts surrounding the use of medicines.

Rising costs and expectations of, and demand for, healthcare are among the most prominent concerns to governments across the globe. Ageing populations and the development of new pharmaceutical technologies are major contributory factors. Ensuring cost-effective provision and delivery remain high on the political agendas of countries throughout the world.

Chronic disease (especially cardiovascular disease, diabetes, obesity) has been highlighted by the World Health Organization (WHO) as a major threat to public health. Although chronic disease is not included explicitly in the Millennium Development Goals (see below), it is becoming an increasing global concern, not only in industrialised countries but also in developing countries, where it is in some cases overtaking infectious disease as the principal cause of mortality (Abegunde *et al.*, 2007). Modification of lifestyle (healthy eating, exercise, etc.) is viewed as a vital part of any response to these epidemics. Concerted action by governments in health protection and health promotion activities by the healthcare sector and all health professionals are viewed as important (Gaziano *et al.*, 2007). Pharmacy services, as well as other community-based practitioners in many countries throughout the world, are well-placed to contribute to these activities. In particular, their presence within local communities may enable effective responses which take account of local environmental, social and cultural circumstances.

The lack of an appropriately placed and skilled workforce has been recognised as a major problem for healthcare, especially in the less and least developed countries where, arguably, needs are greatest (WHO, 2006). Movement of health professionals (although less so for pharmacists) has been the subject of national and international research (FIP, 2006). While some local and national actions may be possible to mitigate these problems, the issue is one of global concern and a responsibility of all nations. Counterfeit medicines, similarly, while still principally a problem of less developed countries where it has huge consequences for healthcare, is increasingly in evidence in industrialised countries (Campling and Taylor, 2006). It is recognised that concerted international action is likely to be most effective.

The rational use of medicines, especially in developing countries, has been central to the WHO agenda since the 1980s. Countries within different regions of the world share many features in terms of the availability and use of medicines (WHO, 2004). Many studies have highlighted the ineffective, unsuitable, suboptimal or unsafe prescribing, supply and/or consumption of pharmaceutical products. The importance of equal and equitable patient access to pharmaceuticals has also received international recognition (UN Millennium Project, 2005). From the point of view of any international approach, countries within particular regions of the world or with similar levels of development share many of these features. There have been numerous policies to address problems of irrational use of medicines, of varying levels of effectiveness. What is notable is that these initiatives have tended to focus on health provision in the public sector and many private practitioners, including pharmacists, have been peripheral at best, but usually excluded. However, across the globe, patterns of provision of healthcare are becoming more diverse and inclusive of practitioners in different settings, with skill-mix in the formal and informal sectors. It is increasingly important that all health professionals identify and evaluate their potential contributions to healthcare in the context of international public health needs and policy priorities.

International development is high on the global political agenda. This is seen as a responsibility of the international community. In 2000 the Millennium Development Goals provided a focus for international development agendas. These comprise a series of eight goals (and 18 associated targets) to be achieved by 2015. It is accepted that their achievement depends on international commitment and co-operation (World Bank, 2004). By adopting these goals the international community accepted not only that global responses were required, but that they must also be inter-sectoral and interdisciplinary. While the principal focus of the goals is eradicating poverty and securing improved quality of life for the world's poorest people, they also necessarily span all aspects of public policy: education, gender equality, environmental sustainability, governance and global partnerships in trade (including specific reference to issues in medicines and health such as 'orphan drugs' and intellectual property rights). Thus, although just three of the goals are specifically health-related, issues around health and pharmaceuticals in different ways are important to the achievement of all (www.un.org/millenniumgoals).

Supply, access to and administration of medicines for infectious diseases, especially antiretrovirals, antimalarials, antibiotics and vaccines, are prominent concerns of the international community. This is both in terms of combating existing high-fatality diseases and being prepared to contain new ones (e.g. avian 'flu) that could become a wide-spread threat. Global and regional responses are clearly necessary (Anderson, 2004).

In addition to recognising the importance of international collaboration to address issues of concern in healthcare and the use of medicines, the complexity of problems will often also require an interdisciplinary approach. For example, use of health services, including pharmacy and medicines, will be in the context of local systems of provision, health beliefs, cultural traditions and individuals' perspectives and preferences regarding the appropriateness of different courses of action and use of drugs (Payer, 1996). To ensure local relevance, an international collaboration must also take into account the wishes and priorities of local stakeholders (Rosser *et al.*, 1997).

The interdependence between nations, and the need for co-operative and concerted actions to achieve mutually beneficial goals, is very apparent. An important goal of international research is to inform and facilitate this.

Why aspire to international research?

In terms of the use and provision of health services and medicines, and the roles (and potential roles) of health professionals, there are many common issues facing governments and populations across the world. Many will be most effectively conceptualised and addressed within an international context. Engagement on an international level indicates an awareness of the relevance and potential value of a global perspective. Hence, the case for an international approach may be strong.

An international perspective may also help inform the research agenda, enabling the identification of factors that may be important determinants or contextual factors. It may also provide an opportunity to increase our appreciation of the diversity of differing perspectives in conceptualising and addressing a research question. In terms of execution of a study many projects may be strengthened by an international approach, which enables investigation of different organisational, socio-economic or other background characteristics, and/or the wider application of study findings.

In some situations, international collaboration may help to promote the credibility of research among policymakers or other stakeholders. This may be particularly beneficial in countries in which research into healthcare, medicines use and the practice of professionals is less well accepted. In countries in which such research is not established, an international project may have an important role in supporting the development of local expertise and capacity building.

From the point of view of the researchers themselves, they may have various motives for participating. Involvement in an international study will provide unique opportunities to learn from, and about, others. International collaboration also, usually, widens the understanding of individual researchers and participants regarding the subject or topic area, presenting new values and perspectives, which may impact on how they view their own local or national situation. On both a conceptual and operational level involvement in an international study will also, hopefully, be a challenging and rewarding experience.

This book

This book is intended for researchers aspiring to, or embarking on, an international project into some aspect of health services, medicines use or related issues. The aim is to highlight some of the special considerations in the context of the fundamental principles of research design and execution that are important for the scientific integrity of all studies, whether local, national or international. In addition to these principles the book also draws on the experiences of researchers who have undertaken international research in this field, to illustrate some of the issues and problems that can arise and enable others to learn from these experiences in developing and conducting their own research programmes.

The book is broadly organised according to the stages in planning and conducting a study. The next chapter focuses on setting up a study, devising relevant and feasible objectives, identifying appropriate study design and ensuring appropriate collaborative and communication procedures are in place, all of which will be essential for the success of the research. Ethical considerations of international research projects are discussed in Chapter 3, alongside the requirements and processes for ethical approval that are a requirement in many countries before a study can commence. This can be time-consuming and therefore the requirements must be established early on. The development of instruments (qualitative or quantitative) for the research has to precede the execution of the study, and this is the subject of Chapter 4. Because of the additional complexity of an international study, ensuring the scientific validity and reliability of instruments across settings requires careful preliminary investigation and preparation. If the instruments are not valid or workable, then the data, and subsequent interpretation of findings, cannot be meaningful.

Once the preparatory work has been undertaken, researchers will embark on the execution of the study: sampling and recruitment of participants, data collection, processing and analysis. All of these will raise many theoretical considerations as well as practical and logistical issues during the course of the study, and they are the subjects of Chapters 5, 6 and 7, respectively. Chapter 8 discusses issues regarding the dissemination of study findings and implications at both national and international levels. As the final chapter, it also summarises the main issues and challenges that occur at all stages of the research process in international collaborations and thus concludes the book.

References

Abegunde D O, Mathers C D, Adam T, Ortegon M, Strong K (2007). The burden and costs of chronic disease in low-income and middle-income countries. *Lancet* 370: 1929–1938.

Anderson S (ed.) (2004). *Managing Pharmaceuticals in International Health*. Basel, Boston, Berlin: Birkhauser Verlag.

Campling N, Taylor D (2006). *Trick or Treat*. London: The School of Pharmacy.

FIP (International Pharmaceutical Federation) (2006). *Global Pharmacy Workforce and Migration Report: a Call for Action*. The Hague: FIP.

Gaziano T A, Galea G, Reddy K S (2007). Scaling up interventions for chronic disease prevention: the evidence. *Lancet* 370: 1939–1946.

Payer L (1996). *Medicine and Culture*. New York: Owl Books.

Rosser W W, Culpepper L, Lam C L K, Parkerson G, Poon V, Van Weel C (1997). Guidelines for international collaborative research. *Fam Pract* 14: 330–334.

UN Millenium Project (2005). *Prescription for Healthy Development: Increasing Access to Medicines*. London: Earthscan.

WHO (World Health Organization) (2004). *The World Medicines Situation*. Geneva: WHO.

WHO (World Health Organization) (2006). *Working Together for Health: The World Health Report 2006*. Geneva: WHO.

World Bank (2004). *The Millenium Development Goals for Health*. Washington DC: IBRD.

2

Planning and setting up the research

Careful and thorough preparatory work that takes place at the start of any study is vital to its ultimate success. Investing time and effort in the early days of any project to ensure that aims and objectives are relevant, clear and achievable, that the study design is appropriate, and that methods are feasible, acceptable and will effectively meet the study objectives, are essential to ensuring that the study is scientifically robust and the findings are of relevance and value.

International research will present many additional considerations and challenges over and above those which feature in local and national projects, many of which should be addressed when planning and setting up a project. Besides different languages, these challenges may include differing perspectives on problems and issues which may impact on the relevance of specific study objectives; organisational, environmental or cultural contexts that may affect the acceptability, feasibility and validity of particular methods; and local views regarding the place and value of research. Approaches to ethical issues, expectations regarding the scientific robustness and standards of conduct such as adherence to protocols may also vary. Appropriate procedures for the management of the project and reviewing progress, including clear agreement on the roles and responsibilities of the team lead and its members should also be in place. A lack of attention to these factors early on could potentially undermine the success of any study.

The purpose of this chapter is to discuss the preparatory work that is essential for any study, but highlighting issues that are of particular relevance to international studies. In planning the study and detailing the protocols, the goals of the research team will be to ensure the acceptability and value of the project in different settings, while maintaining its scientific integrity.

Aims and objectives

The aims and objectives of a study specify what the research is to achieve. In general, aims are broad statements indicating the overall goals of the study, while the objectives are specific and measurable and provide clarification on how the aims will be addressed and met.

In all research the importance of a clear statement of aims and objectives is widely acknowledged. It aids in the identification of an appropriate study design and methodology, determines the data that will be required, including the level of detail. Careful thought about how each objective will be addressed helps to ensure that all relevant information is obtained while guarding against the collection of unnecessary data. The objectives will also provide a framework for the analysis.

It is usual at the start of any study to have some idea of the broad aims of the research. The specific objectives may be less clear. Deriving study objectives that have relevance to a range of settings and contexts requires an appreciation of the significant contextual factors or priorities in the different locations. While many issues in healthcare, pharmacy and medicines use may be common across international boundaries, each location will approach a topic from the point of view of its own policy directions, specific organisational factors in the provision of care, and social or cultural contexts surrounding the management of disease, use of medicines etc. (Koop *et al.*, 2002; see also WHO website for country profiles). Opportunities and challenges vary greatly between countries; objectives pertinent to the priorities and practices in one country may be irrelevant in another.

Thus, for a study that spans international boundaries, specifying the aims and objectives will present additional challenges and considerations. Both the similarities between countries in terms of health problems, health policy agendas, priorities, use of medicines, pharmacy services, etc. and the relevant differences must be identified. Nevertheless, one important feature of an international study will be that conducting the project in more than one country adds value, and aims and objectives are thus usually set to include some form of cross-country comparison.

Devising objectives that are mindful of local contexts is essential if the findings are to be universally valuable. An important purpose of the preliminary fieldwork (see below) will be to identify and explore the agendas and contexts of different partners.

Literature review and preliminary fieldwork

A literature review, together with the preliminary fieldwork, leads to the formulation of specific study objectives and study methodology. In international research, this groundwork will extend to the examination of varying perspectives, identifying organisational, situational or other contextual factors that may be important in different countries.

Literature review

A review of published literature should be as comprehensive and systematic as possible. Because of the interdisciplinary focus of research into health, medicines use and professional practice, strategies for reviewing the literature may need to be wide-ranging. Writers from different perspectives, professions and disciplines may have contributed to research and debate on the topic of interest presenting common or diverse views which could enrich the theoretical, conceptual and/or practical framework of the project.

Countries will vary in the availability and standard of appropriate material for inclusion in a literature review. In countries in which there is an established tradition of health services, medicines use and related research, studies of suitable quality and relevance may be easily identified. Unless positive steps are taken to broaden any review of written material, the results of a literature review could be dominated by perspectives and findings relating to a small number of specific settings which may or may not be typical of the situation elsewhere. It may be easy to make assumptions regarding the transferability of priorities and concerns across international boundaries and to miss important perspectives of another location.

In the context of international research, a strategy for a literature review should be devised to support and inform the study by:

- identifying existing knowledge of the subject;
- identifying contextual factors that may impact on the applicability of research findings to different settings;
- identifying differences in research findings between countries, and considering the extent to which they may reflect methodological issues or real differences in the practices of the different settings;
- exploring the methods that have been used by others in different countries and settings, the reported strengths and weaknesses that they presented and use this to inform the selection and development of methods;
- ensuring that the research will contribute to on-going and emerging debates relevant to both international and local settings.

To ensure identification of issues relating to all settings, a search strategy may need to be broadened to include national and local research

PERSONAL ACCOUNT 2.1

TINA BROCK, TANA WULIJI AND DAVID TAYLOR

Obtaining country-level information in an international study on smoking cessation and pharmacy services

---

Initially we were trying to determine whether smoking cessation incentivisation schemes similar to those for pharmacists in the UK might motivate international pharmacists to provide smoking cessation services in other countries, particularly where smoking is most prevalent. However, before we could investigate such a specific topic, we needed a better understanding of current policy and practices at the individual country level. We completed a comprehensive review of the literature, but soon realised that published accounts of tobacco use policy and related pharmacy activities were skewed towards the Western world and did not necessarily reflect practice on the ground. The World Health Organization (WHO) provided numerical data about tobacco use for each country and the World Bank gave estimates for the value of different interventions (e.g. use bans, education) but no one source had specific details about the services being offered by pharmacists in different countries, which meant we had to collect this information ourselves country-by-country. Due to language barriers, we were also limited to countries with reports published in English.

Realising these limitations, we partnered with the International Pharmaceutical Federation (FIP), using their Global Network of Pharmacists Against Tobacco to identify pharmacists in each of the constituent countries who not only had experience with smoking cessation services but were also involved with local policy development. Speaking and communicating by e-mail with these pharmacists directly allowed us to learn more about their experiences and developments in this area as well as openly probe specifics about the readiness of their consumers, their health professionals and their governments for pharmacist-led smoking cessation services.

From their reports, it was clear that there were different stages of policy and practice development and that local culture strongly influenced attitudes toward smoking cessation service provision. Depending upon the stage of development, these attitudes could serve as barriers or ameliorators to policy development. Ultimately, we concluded that while some aspects of the UK pharmacist incentivisation programme might be transferable to other countries, the mechanisms for the development of policies to support such schemes varied widely.

Some of the lessons learned about the research process are that when investigating international policy:

- One may find only limited information in the published literature.
- Biases (or lack of understanding of local culture) might lead one to miss or misinterpret important factors.

- Partnering with a well-connected organisation can help to identify local sources.
- These 'in country' sources can help to explain not only local policy (the laws) but also how these policies are actually implemented (the practices).

Reference

Brock T P, Taylor D G, Wuliji T (2007). *Ending the Global Tobacco Pandemic*. Policy paper 4. The School of Pharmacy, University of London. London, UK.

and professional journals, local newsletters, policy documents, abstracts from local conferences, etc. In their personal account, concerning the research process when investigating international health policy, Tina Brock and colleagues describe a strategy used to obtain an accurate picture of policy and practice regarding smoking cessation and pharmacy services at individual country level (Personal account 2.1). They highlight the importance of identifying local sources and understanding local cultural factors to interpret and explain information regarding local policy and practices.

Critical appraisal is an important part of any literature review (Greenhalgh, 2001). While quality may vary, it is important that material that provides insights into the applicability of the research to different settings is included. A search strategy and criteria for inclusion of material may need to be tailored to each site. It may be possible for local investigators to seek out relevant material. For this the search strategy may need to be inclusive and wide-ranging. For example, the research team may want to consider the potential impact of restricting the literature review to only English (or any other) language papers. Access to sources in different languages may be required, which may involve all team members and/or assistance from other researchers or stakeholders with knowledge of the individual language and ideally also national databases and other search strategies. Furthermore, international databases such as MEDLINE and EMBASE list English abstracts for full papers written in other languages, which could be made accessible with the help of native speakers.

Possible sources of information include:

- Electronic databases
- Citations in key papers
- Hand searches of selected journals
- Unpublished studies

PERSONAL ACCOUNT 2.2
CHUENJID KONGKAEW

Undertaking a systematic review: including papers written in languages other than English

---

Background to the study

Because of my curiosity about the prevalence rate of hospital admissions associated with drug-related problems, I chose to conduct a systematic review and meta-analysis of hospital admissions associated with adverse drug reactions, adverse drug events and medication errors (Kongkaew *et al.*, 2006). Unlike narrative reviews, systematic reviews use explicit and rigorous methods to identify, critically appraise, and synthesise relevant studies.

My reasons for deciding against restriction to English only

I decided to include all articles without any language restrictions because I wanted to avoid language bias. Language bias may lead to overestimation of the prevalence of drug-related problems. English is the predominant language in contemporary medical research, and too often the search strategy for a systematic review or meta-analysis restricts itself to the English language only. Authors outside the English-speaking world who want their work to be recognised have little choice but to attempt to publish in English because these papers are likely to have a greater international impact. In addition, authors whose language is not English may be more likely to publish positive findings in an English language journal, whereas negative findings may be more likely to be published in non-English language journals.

How I went about it

To retrieve relevant articles, I used electronic databases (MEDLINE, EMBASE, CINAHL), which list English abstracts; I also searched the reference sections of all retrieved articles. Studies included in my reviews involved six different languages: English, French, German, Norwegian, Spanish and Portuguese. This meant I needed help with translations, and I used two approaches: translation software and translators who were bilingual in English and one of the relevant languages and who worked in the area of pharmacy. I started by approaching colleagues within my research group who were either able to help me with translations themselves, or referred me to relevant contacts outside of the group (snowballing). Being able to meet with colleagues on site was much easier, as we could sit down together and I could guide them through the information to check whether papers met the review's inclusion criteria. To aid this process with people who were further afield, I used translation software and then asked them to check the accuracy of the translation and my conclusions as to inclusion or exclusion of the study.

Challenges

The main challenge was seeking assistance with translations from other people. This could be onerous on them, especially if we could not go through papers together. However, the availability of an English abstract and the use of translation software meant I could do quite a bit of the assessment myself and could then guide translators through specific queries, thus reducing their time commitment.

Benefits

There have been benefits at both a scientific and personal level. Using translations has meant I could include non-English papers in my review, thus achieving my aim of reducing language bias. At a personal level, it has greatly enhanced my networking skills and enabled contacts with colleagues I would otherwise not have experienced.

Reference

Kongkaew C, Ashcroft, D M, Noyce, PR (2006). Hospital admissions associated with adverse drug reactions: a meta-analysis of prospective observational studies. In: *Proceedings of the 12th Health Services Research and Pharmacy Practice Conference, Bath 2006*, p. 53.

- Local, national and international conference abstracts
- Reports by policy-bodies, statements of policy
- Reports or discussion papers from stakeholder groups or other interested organisations
- Correspondence in the media, highlighting relevant issues of concern
- Other unpublished work, e.g. discussions at seminars.

In her personal account of undertaking a systematic review, Chuenjid Kongkaew describes her rationale and approach to a multi-lingual review, highlighting the challenges and benefits of taking the extra steps to include research papers written in languages other than English (Personal account 2.2).

Preliminary fieldwork

Preliminary fieldwork refers to those activities that are undertaken in the planning stages of a study to refine the objectives, inform the methodology and to prepare a detailed study protocol. Preliminary field-work complements the review of the literature by providing additional background information. In each setting, it enables identification and examination of the topic in local contexts. For example, it may be designed to examine specific gaps in evidence regarding the relevance and feasibility of the research in specific settings or contexts, the extent to which priorities, concerns or practices cross-international boundaries, or the likely acceptability and effectiveness of proposed study procedures in all study sites.

Thus, an important goal of the preliminary fieldwork is to examine the topic from the perspective of all stakeholders and ensure that their thoughts and concerns are taken into account in the development of the protocol. In research in medicines use and related health issues, the perspectives of consumers, policymakers and health professionals (practitioners) may be important to the research objectives and provide insights into the suitability of methods. In fact, in the UK, and many other countries, there is an increasing emphasis on user involvement in both healthcare policy formation and research (Boote *et al.*, 2002). Indeed, a statement on how, and at what levels, users (patients) are involved is sometimes a requirement when submitting a study protocol for ethical review.

Preliminary fieldwork commonly comprises informal discussions with representatives of stakeholder groups and/or selected individuals identified as having particular experience or expertise. It may include a review of any existing data or documents that will provide an indication of local situations and practices relevant to the study objectives. Sometimes a more structured approach may be taken, in which preliminary data are gathered to explore the perspectives of the population or other interested parties, or to provide information to guide decisions regarding methodology.

In international studies, the range, profile and perspectives of stakeholders in each location should be separately assessed. As different people (project team members or not) may be involved in this exploration and assessment, communication amongst the team to feed this information into the agreed aims and objectives and further stages is crucial. This will help to avoid mistaken assumptions about the importance of issues in different settings, the acceptability of methods and ignorance regarding local concerns and agendas.

The literature review and preliminary fieldwork commonly result in a study protocol which usually includes a clear statement of aims and objectives and stipulates the procedures for the execution of the research.

Advisory groups

The formation of an advisory group could be considered. An advisory group will usually comprise individuals selected for their specific areas of expertise or experience in addition to members of a research team. In an international study, especially one with a number of participants, the research team may already possess a wide range of knowledge and skills, and the establishment of a separate advisory group may not be considered worthwhile or necessary. However, outside input can provide the research team with an opportunity to examine the perspectives of a range of stakeholder groups perhaps representing different study locations. However, convening such a group for an international study, where all members meet in a single location, could be very costly, and alternative methods of consultation may be preferred. In the context of an international study, an advisory group may help in:

- ensuring that objectives are relevant to the topic in the different settings and enabling exploration and discussion of how countries may differ in their perspectives regarding the pertinence of the broad aims of the research study or specific objectives;
- providing information on the perspectives of particular stake-holders, in their own setting, profession or country;
- commenting on, and reviewing, documentation, e.g. information leaflets or data collection forms, in terms of their likely workability and acceptability to potential participants in different settings;
- reviewing the progress of a project; this may include assisting in identifying the reasons for any problems, and suggesting ways of addressing them, either in general or difficulties relating to specific study locations;
- assisting in developing strategies for the dissemination of findings and promoting their uptake in local, national or international contexts.

An advisory group will usually meet periodically throughout the study. Meetings will be planned so that the research team can benefit from advice at key stages of the research. These may typically be in the planning stages: to ensure comment on study objectives, proposed methods and documentation with regard to particular settings or population groups; following pilot work: to address any specific problems, consider how procedures might be refined to improve their acceptability or effectiveness; following data collection and/or on study completion. In an international study, procedures should be agreed for separate review of progress at each site, and relevant decisions communicated to all team members.

Pilot studies

A pilot study serves two principal functions. First, it enables an examination of the acceptability and feasibility of study procedures in representative settings, and secondly, it allows the research team to check that the data obtained will satisfy the study objectives (Smith, 2005).

Are the methods acceptable and workable?

In an international study, acceptability and workability of methods may not be transferable across settings. The feasibility of procedures may be a consequence of differing systems, practices and cultures, and will be reflected in the completeness, reliability and validity of the data. Varying response rates may be an indication of how workable recruitment procedures are in different locations. Patterns of missing or incomplete data may signify an inability or unwillingness to provide information in some settings. Data collection procedures which work well in one place may produce unreliable or incomplete information in another. For example, non-participant observation (covert or overt) may be more acceptable in some places than others. This may be a consequence of practical issues where space is limited or cultural considerations, where in some settings it may be viewed as an invasion of privacy. Thus, a separate assessment of the acceptability and workability of methods should be made for the different study locations.

It is common following a pilot study to consider modifying study procedures to improve their acceptability and hence data quality. In an international study, the differential impact of any modifications across locations must be carefully assessed and will require adequate communication and agreement. This is particularly important in ensuring that comparability of datasets from different study locations is maintained.

Will the data meet the study objectives?

This is the second question addressed by a pilot study. It involves an evaluation of the amount (number of cases), completeness, reliability, validity and generalisability of data. This assessment of the quality of data should also include some site-specific evaluations, to enable any differences between settings to be identified. For example, incomplete datasets may result in bias in study findings. Where the profile of any bias differs between settings, this may jeopardise the comparability of data from different locations and the validity of combining datasets.

Ethical issues

Health services researchers recognise the need to observe high ethical standards in the conduct of their research, and the need for external approval is widely recognised. International guidelines have been developed, however how they are operationalised in different countries varies greatly. Obtaining ethical approval for research within a single country can be time-consuming and consequently costly. In addition to review by an ethics committee, permission may also have to be sought from other bodies, e.g. health authorities, professional or commercial bodies, the universities hosting the research, etc. In an international study, the task of obtaining ethical approval is compounded by the fact that there is huge variation between countries in the requirements and that within countries these requirements are continually changing.

In most studies, appropriate approval has to be obtained prior to commencement of any data collection. The requirements and procedures must be clarified in the early stages and adequate time (often several months) allowed for approval to be obtained, so this topic is mentioned here. However, because in international studies obtaining ethical approval and permission from any other bodies is a major task in conducting research, the following chapter in this book is dedicated to this topic.

A scientific approach

Key considerations important to the scientific integrity of research into healthcare, medicines use and professional practice are study design, generalisability, reliability and validity. Careful attention to these issues will greatly enhance the scientific robustness and ultimate value of the research. Selecting an appropriate design (e.g. according to whether the study is descriptive or experimental) and following associated design principles can be tricky in international research, where applying a common methodology may be thwarted by local conditions. The concepts of generalisability, reliability and validity are important to all stages of the research process: sampling and recruitment, development and choice of instruments, data collection and analysis, where they arise in different ways. Although each of these concepts will be revisited in

future chapters, a brief introduction to these terms, and their importance, may be helpful here.

Study design

The study design will be determined by the aim and objectives which
may be either descriptive, e.g. to document or describe a situation,
professional practices, patients' experiences, or other phenomena; or
evaluative, e.g. to compare phenomena between groups or settings
(including experimental, quasi-experimental, before-and-after, comparative designs); or evaluate an intervention (Cresswell 2003, 2007;
Bowling and Ebrahim, 2005). The aim of the study as either descriptive
or experimental has important implications for sampling strategy. In a
descriptive study a single sample is drawn from a total population
(which may be stratified or clustered). In an experimental study, the
sampling strategy must be devised to enable comparison between
'equivalent' groups. This is discussed in more detail in Chapter 5.

In terms of design, studies may also be cross-sectional or longitudinal (cohort) studies. A cross-sectional study is one in which data are
collected on a single occasion or relating to a particular time period. In
a longitudinal study data are gathered from the same individuals on
repeated occasions over a period of time. Many descriptive studies are
cross-sectional (e.g. a population survey, or series of interviews to document people's views or experiences). Longitudinal studies are common
in intervention studies in which the research team wishes to assess the
impact of an intervention over a period of time.

In general, cross-sectional studies are quicker and easier to
conduct. Studies that require individuals to be followed up may be more
challenging in terms of recruitment (initial response rates) and attrition
(loss of individuals from subsequent phases of data collection). Loss of
individuals to follow-up and/or a decline in commitment of participants
can jeopardise the success of the research. The difficulties of maintaining a sustained commitment from participants and subsequent follow-
up to ensure acceptable response rates can be costly. Also, in a cohort
study, as a consequence of the longitudinal study design, there are
typically lengthy periods before findings are available.

Randomised controlled trials (RCTs) are considered the 'gold
standard' for the evaluation of an intervention. They have additional
requirements for their operation – notably the randomisation of participants to intervention and control groups. In an international study, the
complexities of an experimental study will greatly add to the challenges

of ensuring and maintaining a scientific approach as well as to the project management. In an international context, an RCT is an ambitious undertaking. In Personal account 2.3, Carmel Hughes describes the study design and setting up of an RCT involving pharmacies across seven European countries. This was the first large-scale multi-centre study to be conducted in community pharmacies and co-ordinated in this way.

PERSONAL ACCOUNT 2.3

CARMEL HUGHES

Setting up a randomised controlled trial in seven European countries: providing pharmaceutical care in community pharmacies

The role of medication is central in managing chronic disease. This is particularly exemplified in older people (conventionally taken as those over the age of 65 years) who are prescribed more drugs than younger people and often have a number of co-morbidities. This increases the potential for a range of drug-related problems, a number of which may be resolved through pharmaceutical care delivered by pharmacists. However, this type of intervention had not been tested before and was the impetus for the development of an international study which was conducted in community pharmacies in seven European countries.

The aim of the study (Bernsten *et al.*, 2001) was to assess the impact of a co-ordinated community pharmacy-based pharmaceutical care programme for older patients on a range of health and economic outcomes. The study was a randomised controlled trial performed over 18 months, with data being collected at baseline, 6, 12 and 18 months. Participating community pharmacies from each of the seven countries were randomly assigned as intervention (delivering pharmaceutical care) or control (providing usual services). Pharmacists in both arms of the study were responsible for recruiting patients over the age of 65 years who were receiving four or more prescribed medicines. The intervention provided by pharmacists at the intervention sites focused on educating patients about their medicines and medical conditions, implementing compliance-improving strategies, and rationalising and simplifying drug regimens in collaboration with the patient's general practitioner (GP). In order to perform interventions, pharmacists were required to gather information from the patient, the patient's GP and to use pharmacy held records.

The original idea was generated through an organisation called Pharmaceutical Care Network Europe (PCNE) which was founded in 1994. PCNE was established with the express aim of stimulating the implementation of pharmaceutical care and related research in Europe and

continued overleaf

Personal account 2.3 (continued)

consists of researchers from 17 European countries. Researchers who were interested in collaborating in such a study were identified and drawn from Denmark, Germany, the Netherlands, Northern Ireland (co-ordinating centre), Portugal, the Republic of Ireland and Sweden. The study was the first large-scale, multi-centred, randomised controlled trial to be conducted in community pharmacies in this co-ordinated way.

In order to perform the study, it was necessary to secure funding. This was obtained from the European Commission under the BIOMED 2 programme for medical research. An application was developed jointly between the participating countries which entailed a protocol describing the study, details of all participating centres and researchers, and important milestones and deliverables from the project. Importantly, any funding secured from the BIOMED 2 programme would only support concertation and co-ordination of the study, e.g. development of study materials, travel to attend meetings, but not the actual day-to-day running of the study in each participating country. Hence, each centre had to secure a separate funding stream to hire research staff that would be responsible for recruitment and selection of community pharmacists, training in data collection and data analysis. This proved a major challenge in some countries in which research funding was scarce and research in community pharmacy was not usually undertaken. However, funding was secured from the BIOMED 2 programme and all participating countries managed to attract some funding to support the project in their respective countries.

A large study manual to guide the researchers, and which provided information on the study protocol, all data collection forms and educational material for participating pharmacists and patients, was prepared. This manual had to be translated into native languages and then back-translated into English for checking. In some cases, some selected outcome measures, e.g. the SF 36, a measure of health-related quality of life, were already translated and validated in a number of languages. There were also differences in pharmacy practice and organisation across the participating countries. For example, pharmacies in Sweden were very large, and did not routinely keep computerised patient medication records; in contrast, pharmacies in Northern Ireland were somewhat smaller and did keep such records. These contextual differences had to be accepted, and did help to explain some of the differences in findings between countries.

Project management was central to the success of this project and regular meetings between the participating researchers (usually every six months) helped ensure that we adhered to the timetable as far as possible. However, a number of countries were not able to recruit the required number of patients and this was attributed to lack of interest on the part of patients and their unfamiliarity with pharmacists delivering this kind of service within a research framework.

Although the project findings were equivocal in terms of assessing the impact of pharmaceutical care delivery by community pharmacists, valuable lessons were learned about the management of such a large multi-centre and complex project. We observed that there was probably too much data collection undertaken; outcome measures needed to be simple, reliable and valid; greater multidisciplinary working with other healthcare professionals (notably GPs) may have helped with recruitment. These lessons have been applied to many of our other studies.

The most positive aspect of the study was working with a group of enthusiastic and committed researchers who shared a common goal. We all gained a valuable insight into pharmacy practice in a number of other countries, and perhaps the real measure of success is that we have continued to work together on other projects which seek to demonstrate the value of pharmaceutical care through rigorous research.

Reference

Bernsten C, Bjorkman I, Caramona M, Crealey G, Frokjaer B, Grundberger E, Gustafsson T, Henman M, Herborg H, Hughes C M, McElnay J C, Magner M, van Mil F, Schaeffer M, Silva S, Sondergaard B, Sturgess I, Tromp D, Vivero L, Winterstein A on behalf of the PEER group (2001). Improving the well-being of elderly patients via community pharmacy based provision of pharmaceutical care. *Drugs Aging* 18: 63–77.

Generalisability (external validity)

Generalisability refers to the applicability of the research findings beyond the study participants themselves. It refers to the accuracy with which the results, based on a sample of individuals or cases, can be applied to the study population (i.e. the population from which the sample was drawn). However, a researcher may also want to draw inferences regarding the likely applicability of the work to settings or populations beyond the actual study population. While there may be no statistical basis for this, the researchers may believe, and argue, that the work would be expected to have relevance to other population groups, settings or contexts. The issue of generalisability is discussed in greater detail, and with regard to multi-centre and international studies, in Chapter 5.

Reliability

This concerns the reproducibility of the results and depends on the consistency in the interpretation and use of study measures and procedures. Many stages of the research process involve steps for which the reliability may be questioned. In each case, some assessment of the reliability should be attempted. It is important that processes and methods are objective: independent of the perspectives of the researchers or the research process. In an international study, this may present additional problems in that data will be gathered in different settings, by different people, sometimes using procedures that vary between settings to ensure that they are workable. Identifying and addressing potential problems of reliability in the research process are discussed in subsequent chapters (see Chapters 4, 6 and 7).

Validity

This refers to the 'truth' of the findings. Are the findings an accurate reflection of the phenomena under study? This is subtly different from reliability which is concerned with consistency in the application of measures and methods rather than whether they provide a true picture of the events or situations of interest. While there is some overlap in the questions of reliability and validity, it is useful to separate out these two concepts to address issues of the scientific integrity of the research processes and findings. It is the case that reliability is a prerequisite for validity: if measures are unreliable or procedures are inconsistently applied the findings cannot be an accurate representation of the issues of interest. However, there are situations when reliability may be achieved when validity is not. These issues are discussed further in Chapter 4.

There may also be trade-offs between the reliability and validity. For example, in multi-centre, especially international studies it is important that datasets from the different sites are comparable. Study procedures and instruments (questions and measures) must be similar. However, this may require some compromises where the cross-cultural validity of measures may be questionable, or in attempts to ensure that a survey includes questions of equal relevance in different locations (see Chapter 4).

Defining the aims and identifying the specific objectives of a study is the first major problem or threat to the validity of the work. Identifying a broad aim of international relevance may be relatively straightforward. However, ensuring and that the specific objectives are cognisant of the surrounding issues, i.e. equally relevant and therefore valid in a wide range of settings, is less easy.

Project management and communication

Project management is a major component of any research study, even those that are in a single setting and are a relatively modest undertaking.

Good organisational skills and meticulous record-keeping is central to the smooth running of any project. Notes regarding conceptual frameworks which underpin the research and the development of the methodology must be maintained. These provide a basis for subsequent decisions on the execution of the research. Careful documentation relating to the recruitment of participants, data collection and the operation of the study in each location is necessary for quality assurance, to monitor the extent to which study protocols are followed and to assess the completeness, reliability and validity of data. The value of a detailed 'project manual' is emphasised by James McElnay in Personal account 7.1 (see page 128). Detailed instructions on all aspects of conduct of the project are essential for a consistent application of procedures and ultimate confidence in the research findings.

It is to be expected that a multi-centre study that crosses international boundaries will present greater administrative challenges. In an international study, the management process involves the co-ordination of a number of researchers or research teams. Leading such a project to a successful conclusion will be a skilled task. Central to effective project management leading to successful research is communication between participants. This is highlighted in the personal accounts of many contributors throughout this book. Researchers are generally agreed regarding the importance of detailed discussion prior to the commencement of any project, but participants in different centres will have their own thoughts about the direction, goals and implementation of the project. While it is essential that all voices are heard, participants must also be prepared to compromise to achieve a common goal.

Experienced researchers will be used to making decisions regarding their research and solving problems that arise. In a collaborative project, the level of autonomy, and ways in which discretion can be exercised (e.g. administrative tasks versus decisions on the direction and operation of the research) should be clear. Once the project is underway, systems need to be in place for discussing possible modification to protocols to address any local (or wider) difficulties so that scientific integrity is maintained. Some centres, depending on their expertise and/or capacity, may take greater responsibility for guidance and decisions regarding particular aspects of the study.

In an international project, effective communication includes both issues of comprehension by people who are not native speakers of whatever languages are employed by the research team, as well as adequate processes for exchange of views and ideas between team members. Communication channels should ensure that there is sufficient opportunity for all participants to contribute to decision-making. Positive efforts to identify, explore and acknowledge personal, local and collective perspectives will also help guard against unvoiced agendas, and misplaced assumptions regarding the purpose of the research, autonomy over the process, ownership of data, and use of resources and costs. It is therefore recommended to ensure all decisions that need to be taken, following adequate discussion amongst all team members, are (formally) agreed and recorded (in writing) and distributed to all participants in a timely manner.

Resources

In the planning stages of any project, a realistic assessment of the resources required needs to be made. Even if members of the research team propose to undertake the work (e.g. a pilot study) within their normal daily activities, or as part of a higher degree, a convincing assessment of the workload should be made. The burden and costs of a project can be seriously underestimated. They include activities of project management as well as the execution of the research: recruitment of participants, data collection and analysis, maintenance of records and other documentation, preparation of reports and dissemination of findings. Accordingly, a combination of funding streams may often cover different parts of the project, e.g. a combination of European Union (EU) funding for aspects of project management and communication (travel), and funding from national bodies for the actual conduct of the study in each location.

The research team may be a self-selecting group of enthusiastic individuals who have their own personal motives for participating and expect minimal reimbursement of their time and efforts. But, the roles and expectations of members of the research team should be clear and reasonable. The extent to which individuals will be expected to undertake research activity as part of their work rather than receiving expenses and/or payments, or employing others should be discussed to ensure that this will be acceptable and workable for all. If demands of the research are too high, this could result in non-completion of the project in some or all centres.

Issues of equity in allocation of resources may arise. Payment/salary structures may vary between countries. Some centres may assume a greater administrative burden. Some activities may be more costly in some places than others. The allocation of any project 'overheads' may have to be agreed, and again there may be varying requirements and conventions in different institutions.

Individuals recruited as study participants may or may not expect payment. Offering incentives to prospective participants may be normal practice in some locations or situations, but viewed as unacceptable in others. Practices regarding incentives to prospective participants to achieve higher response rates may differ between centres. Incentives can also have an impact on issues such as response bias.

There may also be logistical considerations in ensuring that all centres have timely access to funds. Both access and allocation must be seen to be fair. A mechanism for review and audit of funds may be required, including procedures or contingencies should there be unforeseen expenditure or over-spends. Mara Guerreiro, in Personal account 2.4, illustrates a case of enthusiastic researchers, collaborating on a project which, without outside resources, became too demanding.

PERSONAL ACCOUNT 2.4

MARA PEREIRA GUERREIRO

Reflections on a collaborative study between six European countries

The research project 'Drug-related problems identified by European community pharmacists in patients discharged from hospital' was developed from a research course organised by the European Society of Clinical Pharmacy (ESCP). This course, which was targeted at practitioners with little experience in research, took place in Reykjavik in 2000, coupled with the 1st ESCP Spring Conference on Clinical Pharmacy. In addition to developing clinical pharmacists' research skills, ESCP aimed to develop a trans-national research network. As a result, participants were expected to design a research protocol and to conduct the study in their countries under the supervision of the course tutors.

Course participants were split into groups according to the setting where they practised – I was part of the community pharmacy group. Early in the course we were presented with possible research topics and their rationales; my group chose to pursue work on drug-related problems in patients discharged from hospital. During the four days, lectures were alternated with group work, moderated by the tutors. By the end of the course we had developed a first draft of the study protocol, which was later refined. Our objectives were to examine the nature and frequency of drug-related problems in community pharmacies among patients discharged from hospitals and to examine several variables relating to these drug-related problems.

continued overleaf

Personal account 2.4 (continued)

Members of the research group acted as co-ordinators in their countries, and were in charge of operationalising the study. This involved not only recruiting participants and overseeing data collection but also liaising with the two study co-ordinators, based in a Dutch pharmacy practice research institute. Although this was a successful organisational model, a number of practical problems arose, mainly related with project management:

- No budget was allocated to the research project, which had implications in terms of material and human resources. For example, procedures for claiming expenses associated with the research process (e.g. printing and mailing) were never clearly communicated. Instead of assuming that country co-ordinators would turn to the sponsor organisation (ESCP) or to the study co-ordinators for reimbursement, it would have been more efficient for all parts involved to make procedures clear from the outset. Additionally, researchers were expected to sacrifice their own time to the project. This may seem reasonable, as it was a learning opportunity for pharmacists relatively inexperienced in research, but it is not without disadvantages. Accumulating research activities on top of daily practice proved to be overly demanding in some cases. A few of the original research group members were unable to sustain participation in the project and substitutes had to be found. One explanation is the lack of recognition of the work involved due to pharmacists' inexperience in research. In future it may be worth providing realistic estimates of the time involved in participation and encouraging teaming-up with other researchers in each country to share tasks. Another disadvantage of relying on researchers' good will was that compliance with deadlines was troublesome, as tasks tended to be done when it was possible to fit them in. Delays, especially when it came to reporting and submitting findings for publication, were solved by including a final year pharmacy student in the project. At the time the student was doing her training in a community pharmacy in the Netherlands, affiliated with the pharmacy practice research institute.
- Maintaining co-operation from the beginning until findings were disseminated (more than three years later) was challenging. At the start it was planned to use the bi-annual ESCP conferences for face-to-face meetings and e-mail contacts in-between. However, attendance at meetings was limited to the study co-ordinators and one or two other members of the research group; sometimes there was little feedback to e-mails. Moreover, the use of e-mail proved to be inefficient in a number of circumstances, such as when multiple clarifications were required (i.e. time-consuming to write explanations, did not allow debate). Using conference calls was not explored but could have helped to overcome these problems while maintaining motivation. Telephone calls involving several people can nowadays be easily organised at virtually no cost with the aid of information technologies (e.g. Skype).

In hindsight, I feel that we should have employed procedures to ensure accuracy of the data collection instrument translation into different languages and to safeguard its cross-national equivalence. This is especially important since results from different countries were compared. However, at the time the importance of this issue seemed to be overlooked even by journal reviewers, who never inquired or commented about it when assessing publication manuscripts. A growing number of cross-national research projects may have contributed to an increased awareness of these issues.

I found 'Drug-related problems identified by European community pharmacists in patients discharged from hospital' to be a successful research project. The goals established at the outset were achieved and preliminary findings were distinguished with an award for the best poster by the Dutch Health Care Foundation. Furthermore, some of the authors are still in contact nowadays and have worked together on other projects. Nonetheless, I learnt an important lesson about research: to avoid disappointment and frustration it is fundamental to secure funding and researchers' availability and skills.

Reference

Paulino E I, Bouvy M, Gastelurrutia M A, Guerreiro M, Buurma H (2004). Drug-related problems identified by European community pharmacists in patients discharged from hospital. *Pharmacy World Sci* 26: 353–360.

Conclusion

Devoting sufficient time to the planning stages of a project is invaluable and will be a major determinant of its ultimate success. Detailed exploration of differing perspectives of research team members and stakeholders, and careful examination of the feasibility of proposed methods in all locations will greatly improve the chances of the smooth running of the research.

A robust approach in the early stages to identify potential threats to the scientific integrity will ensure that time and money invested in the project result in a high-quality, dependable study. Appropriate management processes, including the agreement on different team members' roles and responsibilities, should be established as these will assist in the early identification of any problems and in monitoring the progress of the project.

In an international project, discussion and agreement between research team members is not only important but also more challenging than in most other projects. Good and regular communication is therefore crucial! This will be achieved through a combination of written (mostly electronic, i.e. e-mail), telephone (one-to-one as well as conference) and face-to-face meetings, and adequate funding to facilitate these needs to be incorporated in the project costings.

References

Boote J, Telford R, Cooper C (2002). Consumer involvement in health research: a review and research agenda. *Health Policy* 61: 213–236.

Bowling A, Ebrahim S (2005). *Handbook of Health Research Methods*. Maidenhead: Open University Press.

Cresswell J W (2003). *Research Design: Qualitative, Quantitative and Mixed Methods Approaches*. London: Sage.

Cresswell J W (2007). *Qualitative Enquiry and Research Design*, 2nd edn. London: Sage.

Greenhalgh T (2001). *How to Read a Paper*. London: BMJ.

Koop C E, Pearson C E, Schwarz M R (eds) (2002). *Critical Issues in Global Health*. San Francisco: Jossey-Bass.

Smith F J (2005). *Conducting your Pharmacy Practice Research Project*. London: Pharmaceutical Press.

3

Ethics in international research

The purpose of this chapter is to discuss the potential ethical issues associated with international research. All research should be conducted in both a scientifically robust and ethically sound manner. Many, but not all, countries therefore have mechanisms to formally review research protocols. Impartial ethical review is designed to minimise physical or social harm to research participants. It also protects participants' rights to privacy and to choose freely whether to participate in research. In addition, ethical review provides a safety net for researchers, institutions and sponsors (Wagner, 2003). For example, ethical approval is often requested before the release of funds from sponsors of research, editors of scientific journals often ask for confirmation of ethical approval, and in drugs trials, regulatory authorities require it.

This chapter begins with an introduction to the principles and guidelines of research ethics. It outlines a description of the functions of research ethics committees and provides an example of a systematic approach to ethical review, including a series of questions that may help to clarify the researcher's thinking at the time of preparing a research protocol. Informed consent, an important requirement, is discussed in some detail. The chapter closes with a summary of the ethical responsibilities for the international researcher.

Principles, approaches and guidelines

The fundamental basis of research ethics is about ensuring that vulnerable people are protected from exploitation and other forms of harm (Schüklenk, 2005). In order for a scientific investigation involving human participants to be universally acknowledged as ethical, two conditions need to be met: a theoretically and methodically sound research design and voluntary informed consent (Marshall, 2005). In international studies additional contextual considerations arise. For example, undertaking research in socio-culturally or economically diverse locations will require a respect for the different approaches to ethical issues which will be in the context of differing priorities, perspectives and environments (Benatar, 2002). In less-developed countries, it will be important that research results relate to the health priorities of the recipient country or to local capacity building, so justifying the best use of scarce resources. There is a wide literature on the place and complexities of research and development (R&D). However, specifically with regard to the topic of this chapter careful consideration of the links between health research and development can make for an intricate ethical situation (Robison, 1998; Olsen *et al.*, 2003).

Michael Heinrich, in his personal account describes the ethnobotanist as a link between diverse cultures which brings with it a diverse combination of ethical considerations (Personal account 3.1). For example, he raises ethical responsibilities that may arise as a consequence of the commercial exploitation of any potential pharmaceutical product in which, of course, the country of origin should benefit financially. More broadly, he highlights the significance of the partnership between 'provider countries' (i.e. of plant material and information on their uses) where knowledge resides, and outside researchers. He emphasises the importance of an appreciation of the place, contexts and consequences of the research process and outcomes for local communities.

A number of key documents have been produced by international bodies to identify ethical principles to research and guide their application with the aim of protecting human participants. The Nuremberg Code (1947) is the first, and historically the most important, international research ethical guideline. In 1964, the first Declaration of Helsinki was published by the World Medical Association, detailing regulations about research involving human subjects; there have since been five revisions, the fifth in Edinburgh (2000). Researchers in the USA are guided by the Belmont Report (1979) which is based on three ethical principles: justice (equal share and fairness), beneficence (the obligation to maximise benefits and minimise harms) and autonomy (respect for persons) (Dresden *et al.*, 2003). In 1991 and 1993 the Council for International Organizations of Medical Sciences (CIOMS, 2002) (founded by the World Health Organization and UNESCO) produced its own guidance for both clinical and epidemiological research (Schüklenk, 2005; Marshall, 2005). A number of other countries and bodies have also published their own sets of guidelines.

Focusing on international research, Salako (2006) described the three main issues highlighted by the Declaration of Helsinki, which is the most widely cited international ethical standard. The first is that researchers must be aware of the ethical, legal and regulatory requirements for research involving human participants in their own countries

PERSONAL ACCOUNT 3.1

MICHAEL HEINRICH

Ethnobotany and ethnopharmacy – multidisciplinary links between partners in developing countries and the 'West'

Pharmaceutical discoveries of the last decades based on the systematic evaluation of higher plants include, for example, camptothecan (and its derivatives), podophyllotoxin, vincristine and paclitaxel – all essential medicines in cancer chemotherapy – and galanthamine, a drug widely used in the symptomatic treatment of Alzheimer's disease (Balick and Cox, 1997; Heinrich and Teoh, 2004). These drugs are all derived from higher plants which were, and are, used by indigenous peoples as medicines. Norman Farnsworth (1990) estimated that 74% of the 119 drugs still derived from higher plants were discovered as the result of ethnobotanical research. Early explorers documented this knowledge and today such studies form one aspect of a multidisciplinary field of research – ethnobotany, defined as the study of the relationship between people and plants. It addresses broad issues of the human use of plants for food, clothing, ornament, ritual, building materials and religious uses. Ethnobotanists take detailed field notes and collect carefully documented plant samples – voucher specimens – that allow for precise determination of the plant species. Selected species are then studied pharmacologically and phytochemically in order to identify the active constituents.

Examples of early studies include those by the German Alexander von Humboldt (1769–1859), who conducted multidisciplinary studies in the Americas, and the French pharmacologist Claude Bernard (1813–1878), who studied the mechanism of action of curare, one of the plants 'discovered' by these explorers (Heinrich *et al.*, 2004). Two of the most famous British botanical explorers were Sir Hans Sloane (1660–1753), who studied plants most notably on Jamaica, and much later Richard Spruce (1817–1893), who worked in South America. In nearly all of these cases stakeholders from two or more countries (or two groups within one country) are involved (e.g. researchers and local informants).

However, while Spruce and von Humboldt simply 'explored' the unknown foreign countries, today the commercial potential of a country's biodiversity puts particular responsibilities on the ethnobotanist who often is a link between two cultures, two countries, and diverse views of understanding and interpreting the world. Such research is now based on mutually binding agreements and it is generally expected that the region or country of origin should receive some financial benefits if a commercially successful product is developed out of such a research collaboration.

continued overleaf

Personal account 3.1 (continued)

More recently the systematic evaluation of indigenous pharmacopoeias in order to contribute to improved healthcare in marginalised regions has come onto the agenda of international and national organisations and of non-governmental organisations (NGOs). The World Health Organization estimates that 85% of the world's population depends directly upon local medicinal plants for medicine. Ethnobotanical and ethnopharmaceutical research can assist developing nations in assessing the safety and efficacy of plants used in traditional herbal medicine. An example is *Artemisia annua*, the source plant of the antimalarial sesquiterpene lactone artemisinin, which is now grown in some African countries and an extract is used in the treatment of malaria (Mueller *et al.*, 2000). This example also raises important questions about the widespread use of such extracts which may contribute to the development of resistance against the active compound. On the other hand, the huge problems with counterfeit 'licensed' medicines calls for solutions which involve local people, and the growing of medicinal plants may well be one such possibility.

In all these cases the original keepers of knowledge reside in what is now called 'provider countries' and thus ethnobotanical and ethnopharmaceutical research owes special debts to these keepers of knowledge, and novel ways of communicating this knowledge to future generations have become essential aspects of ethnobotanical research and practice (e.g. Vandebrock *et al.*, 2003; Rivera *et al.*, 2006). Today, more and more ethnobotanists come from developing countries, but in these cases, too, two cultures or sectors of a society meet.

References

Balick M J, Cox P A (1997). *Plants, People and Culture.* New York: WH Freeman and Co. Scientific American Library.

Farnsworth N (1990). The role of ethnopharmacology in drug development. In: Battersby A, Marsh J (eds) *Bioactive Molecules From Plants* (Ciba Symposium 154). Chichester: Wiley, pp. 2–21.

Heinrich M, Teoh H L (2004). Galanthamine from snowdrop – the development of a modern drug against Alzheimer's disease from local Caucasian knowledge. *J Ethnopharmacol* 92: 147–162.

Heinrich M, Barnes J, Gibbons S, Williamson E M (2004). *Fundamentals of Pharmacognosy and Phytotherapy.* London: Churchill Livingstone (Elsevier).

Mueller M S, Karhagomba I B, Hirt H M, Wemakor E (2000). The potential of *Artemisia annua* L. as a locally produced remedy for malaria in the tropics: agricultural, chemical and clinical aspects. *J Ethnopharmacol* 73: 487–493

Rivera, D, Verde A, Fajardo J, Inocencio C, Obón C, Heinrich M (eds) (2006). *Guía etnobotánica de los alimentos locales recolectados en la provincia de Albacete.* Instituto de Estudios Albacetenses 'Don Juan Manuel' de la Excma. Diputación de Albacete. Alabacete, Spain. Serie Estudios No. 167.

Vandebroek, I, Thomas E, AMETRAC (2003) Plantas medicinales para la atención primaria de la salud. E17 conocimiento de ocho medicos tradicionales de Apillapampa 8 (Bolivia), Ina; Indústrias Gráficas Serrano, Cochabamba (Bolivia).

and any other countries where the research is being undertaken. Second, the research is only justified if there is a reasonable likelihood that the populations in which the research is carried out stand to benefit from the results. Third, negative and positive results should be published or made otherwise publicly available. Within this, potential conflicts of interest should be disclosed: to research ethics committees, to patients when informed consent is sought, and in any research publication.

While these documents have a central role in guiding researchers regarding ethical principles, there is considerable variability in the socio-cultural environments and capabilities of institutions and communities where research is undertaken. Particular challenges may arise in balancing international ethical standards for research with local standards and the pragmatic considerations in carrying out the research. For example, potential conflicts may arise between universal standards and traditional customs for requirements such as informed consent (Marshall, 2005). Rashad et al. (2004) highlighted a range of difficulties that resulted from undertaking a research study in Egypt, for which the research protocol had undergone ethical review in the UK (see Box 3.1).

Rashad's experience illustrated the huge challenges of applying universal ethical principles and practices. When applying ethical guidelines across international boundaries, there is a need to respect each culture within which the study is set. This includes sensitivity to cultural understanding and religious beliefs and attempting to minimise the imbalance of power (which is greater when principal investigators from a more developed country are recruiting participants from a less well-developed country) as this has the potential for exploitation (Olsen et al., 2003; Kennedy et al., 2006).

The importance of research ethics must explicitly include consideration of the community's interests as well as those of the individual (Dresden et al., 2003). Researchers need to be creative in developing strategies to improve participants' understanding of the research aims, methods, risks and benefits. In addition, prompt and continuous feedback to participants and their communities should be carried out in ways that are culturally and linguistically meaningful (Marshall, 2005).

Box 3.1 An example of difficulties associated with imposing UK ethical requirements onto a study carried out in Egypt (taken from Rashad *et al.*, 2004)

- Until 1991, there were no national standardised ethical guidelines that could be applied to healthcare research in Egypt.
- Egypt has a scarcity of research ethics committees.
- Most research takes place within the public teaching hospitals, which are mainly used by patients from lower socio-economic sectors of Egyptian society.
- Egyptian doctors are regarded as a powerful professional group, so a paternalistic approach to care dominates resulting in reduced autonomy for research participants; there is an assumption amongst patients that the doctor will always act in their best interests; patients expect doctors to make decisions for them (influenced by cultural norms and beliefs). Unequal power relationship between health professionals and patients is pronounced in Egypt.
- Decision-making is commonly delegated to the most powerful figure in the context within which the decision is being made, e.g. father, teacher, employer.
- Low literacy levels exist amongst poor, uneducated women, who are frequently used as research participants in Egypt – this has potential implications for these women's abilities to make informed choices about participation.
- Confirmation of informed consent requiring a person's signature presents unique challenges as a signature has particular significance in Egyptian society and is usually only used in relation to major life events. Furthermore, requesting a written signature also implies a lack of trust in one's word.
- A cultural emphasis on politeness could increase an individual's perceived obligation to participate in research.

Conflicts can occur when the values and norms of the study population do not match those of the research team. However, a collaborative approach to setting a research agenda together can help ensure the appropriateness of the work and that limited resources are used to the best advantage of the countries involved. Providing the local community (such as local healthcare staff, community leaders or advocacy agencies) an early opportunity and a continuing mechanism to provide input into the purposes, goals and methods of research, could reduce the opportunities for exploitation in less-developed countries (Robison, 1998; Olsen *et al.*, 2003). However, the valuable involvement of community partners must not compromise the research team's autonomy and ability to ensure that scientific integrity of the research is maintained and ethical principles are observed.

Research ethics committees

Research ethics committees are independent bodies who review research, particularly that involving 'patients', and they exist in many (but not all) developed countries. Benatar (2002) identified three functions of a research ethics committee. The first is the independent evaluation of research proposals: focusing on risk/benefit ratios, distribution of benefits and burdens, potential conflicts of interest, adequacy of information provided for potential research participants and the protection of freedom with regards to participants granting/withdrawing their consent and researchers' rights to publish. Second, they have a role to educate and assist all those involved in the process to understand and appreciate ethics. Third, they have a duty to monitor and audit research, and to provide accountability to the public.

In international research the structures, procedures and requirements for gaining ethical approval can vary significantly between countries. This was demonstrated by Hearnshaw (2004), who compared the processes required to gain ethical committee approval for an identical intervention study which aimed to improve the involvement of older patients in consultations with their general practitioners across 11 European countries (Austria, Belgium, Denmark, France, Germany, Israel, the Netherlands, Portugal, Slovenia, Switzerland and the UK). For example, in the UK, if research takes place involving human participants and/or resources within the UK's National Health Service (NHS), then independent review is sought through the National Research Ethics Service (NRES). In addition, there may be further requirements from other NHS committees and subgroups (e.g. management approval from NHS R&D offices), or institutions hosting the research (e.g. universities). International research undertaken entirely outside the UK (including that by UK-based researchers) is beyond the ethical review remit of the NRES and would require ethical approval in the country where the research will take place. If the research will be undertaken both within the UK and overseas, an NRES would only review the component of the study that actually takes place within the UK. Ethical approval for international studies gained in countries other than the UK does not nullify any requirements for ethical review in the UK, and vice versa (NRES, 2007).

In many countries processes are becoming more advanced and are continually evolving. It is, therefore, important to build the necessary time into a project to establish what is required in each participating country in terms of criteria, supporting documentation and costs, as well as the time it will take for a decision to be made. This can take several months. In her personal account, Mary Tully describes her experience and feelings regarding the differing requirements for independent ethical review for a study conducted in the UK and Sweden; two European countries for which it might be expected that requirements would be similar (Personal account 3.2).

PERSONAL ACCOUNT 3.2

MARY TULLY

Ethics committee approvals between different countries

I had conducted some work in the UK that explored how doctors in different specialities and of different grades viewed how the appropriateness of prescribing should be measured. As part of my visiting professorship to the University of Uppsala, Sweden, I had a new PhD student. Therefore, I had the opportunity to repeat my original work in another country, as views of appropriate prescribing and prescribing documentation may well depend on current healthcare debate and different healthcare systems (Ljungberg et al., 2007).

In the UK, conducting qualitative interviews with hospital doctors, about their own prescribing and about prescribing in general, had required full NHS ethics committee approval, including attending the meeting. The committee had asked me to make amendments to the subject information sheet for the doctors before giving approval. In Sweden, therefore, I expected to have to make an application and, as vice-chair of an NHS committee, was interested to learn about the ethics committee application process in another country. My Swedish collaborators, however, said that research of this kind did not usually require approval. I pressed the matter and said that I would prefer to try even if they thought it was not needed, so that my PhD student (and I) could learn the system. However, I was told that an ethics committee application costs between Kr5000 and Kr16000 (approximately £385–1230), depending on the type of research – even if the committee later said an application had not been required. I did not press the matter any further! I had expected a variation in the system, but being so used to the free NHS ethics service, charging for this never entered my mind.

Reference

Ljungberg C, Kettis Lindblad Å, Tully M P (2007). Hospital doctors' views of factors influencing their prescribing. *J Eval Clin Pract* 13: 765–771.

In countries in which requirements are limited, members of the research team will want to be satisfied that the work is in accordance with accepted principles, that their own expectations regarding ethical standards are met and that they are satisfied that the research has undergone suitable external review and possible frameworks for review are discussed below.

The ethical review process

The independent review of research and its ethical acceptability takes time. The ethical issues in a research project have to be identified and considered. The potential risks and consequences have to be appraised and balanced against the potential benefits and a conclusion has to be drawn about the research as a whole. This often requires a delicate assessment; any decision may not be clear cut. Ideally, careful and reasonable thinking is required by the research ethics committee members who collectively understand the importance of different moral claims, and who can work constructively together to come to sound and reasonable conclusions (Foster, 2001).

A number of systematic frameworks have been developed for the review process. For example, in the USA, based on the Belmont Report, Robison (1998) detailed an ethical review process that focuses on three key features:

- Respect for persons (informed consent; voluntary participation; adequate awareness of benefits and possible risks)
- Beneficence (first do no harm; contribute to the general welfare/ health of study participants)
- Justice (equitable distribution of burdens and benefits of participating in research).

Nicola Gray, a UK-based researcher, discusses in her personal account how when undertaking research in the USA, the Belmont Report represented a new framework for identifying and addressing ethical issues, and how this has continued to provide a stimulus for reviewing her work following her return to the UK (Personal account 3.3).

As a further example of a general framework which may be applied to judge the ethics of a research project, Foster (1996, 2001) highlighted three distinct approaches, together with a series of questions, which may be helpful to reflect upon when preparing a research protocol:

PERSONAL ACCOUNT 3.3
NICOLA GRAY

Undertaking health services research in the USA – ethics

To explore adolescents' views and experiences of using the Internet to find information about health and medicines, our study involved focus group discussions with middle and high-school students in the USA aged 11–18 years (Gray *et al.*, 2005). Ethical review was undertaken by the Research Subjects Review Board (RSRB) within the institution where I was placed for my Fellowship – the University of Rochester Medical Center, New York State. This review board deals with a breadth of research subjects similar to that of a local research ethics committee in the UK. At the time of my study, the chair and vice-chair of the RSRB were both pharmacists – a fact that was apparently common, considering the many drug trials undertaken within these university hospitals.

Key study personnel and any fieldworker who might be called upon to take consent from subjects are required to register with the RSRB. As our study was considered minimal risk, I completed the Ethical Principles in Research Program (EPRP); there is another level for interventions. The EPRP revolves around the Belmont Report (1978). Published in the wake of the Tuskegee syphilis experiment, in which 399 black men were purposely left untreated in order to study the late-stage disease (Jones, 1993), the report considers the difference between practice and research, and crystallises three basic principles of ethical research, which Tuskegee patently ignored, and their application within a research study with human subjects:

Basic principle	Application
Respect for persons	Informed consent
Beneficence	Assessment of risk and benefits
Justice	Selection of subjects

I have found this pithy and thought-provoking report to be invaluable since returning to the UK as a resource for pharmacy students and my own ethics applications.

The RSRB required a score of at least 80% on a short multiple-choice questionnaire submitted to their office. Successful completion resulted in an EPRP registration number being issued, and this had to be quoted for each fieldworker in the subsequent study application. The registration has to be renewed every three years and so, two years after my return, I had to renew my registration with Rochester as I was still analysing and writing up from study data.

After favourable ethical review, the original copies of information sheet and consent form submitted with the application and annotated with version number and date were taken, almost ceremonially, to the RSRB office where they were rubber stamped and signed by a RSRB officer. It was then obligatory to photocopy these documents, complete with stamp and signature, for distribution to potential subjects as verified copies of the original. Luckily the photocopier was in good condition so the quality of the copied leaflets was acceptable!

References

Belmont Report (1978). *Ethical Principles and Guidelines for the Protection of Human Subjects of Research*. DHEW Publication No. (OS) 78–0012.
Gray N J, Klein J D, Noyce P R, Sesselberg T S, Cantrill J A (2005). Health information seeking behaviour in adolescence: the place of the internet. *Soc Sci Med* 60: 1467–1478.
Jones J H (1993). *Bad Blood: The Tuskegee Syphilis Experiment*, expanded edition. New York: Free Press.

- Goal-based approach (validity of the research)
- Duty-based approach (welfare of the research participant)
- Rights-based approach (dignity of the research participant).

In using Foster's approach, equal weight may not always be given to all three and the decision will be based upon which concerns need to take precedence, a judgement made with each individual research project. This approach is discussed in further detail below.

Goal-based approach (validity of the research)

From a goal-based approach, an action is considered good if its goal, or outcome, is good. The outcome of a study cannot be of value (i.e. good) if the work is not conceptually or methodologically sound. Thus, in an ethical appraisal, the scientific merit of the work should be challenged. The research team should be able to defend the study design and methods as a sound approach to answering the research questions, or testing the hypotheses (see Box 3.2).

In the case of vulnerable groups (e.g. children, older people, people with mental health problems or special needs) special consideration must be given to the potential benefits of a study. Is the research necessary in this particular group of individuals, and is this the group who are likely to benefit? Can the results be generalised from the sample or study population to any other groups?

Box 3.2 Questions to ask yourself from a goals-based perspective

- For what reasons is the research being conducted?
- Is the research likely to provide new insights into a social phenomenon?
- How important is the research question?
- Is the research design optimal and will it answer the research questions posed?
- Are the research methods chosen to answer the question appropriate, rigorous and systematically applied?
- Have the data collection tools been tested or justified?
- How will the data be analysed?

Duty-based approach (welfare of the research participant)

The focus of the duty-based approach is whether or not the proposed research activities accord with moral principles. These considerations should take precedence over whether the outcome of the research activity is good. For example, even if a very important question may be answered by the research, it would be deemed unethical to deceive the research participants in order for the research to be undertaken (see Box 3.3).

For therapeutic research, where there are direct health benefits for participants (as compared to non-therapeutic research where there are no direct benefits for participants but there may be future benefits to those meeting the same inclusion criteria) the concept of *equipoise* should be considered (Choudhury and Knapp, 2006). For therapeutic research to be considered ethical, the participant must expect to receive treatment which is at least as good as the treatment they would have received had they not been enrolled in the research. That is, the new

---

Box 3.3 Questions to ask yourself from a duty-based perspective

- What will participating in the research involve?
- In what ways will the research participants be treated?
- How much time might participating in the study involve?
- How intrusive might the interview or questionnaire be?
- What will happen to the information that is collected?
- To what risks will the research participants be exposed?
- Are the risks necessary and acceptable in the circumstances?
- Are there referral procedures to appropriate agencies in place if information that leaves an individual at risk, is revealed?

---

treatment must be considered to be at least as good as 'the usual' treatment. Equally, the researcher must be uncertain whether the treatment that is being tested is actually better than standard or 'usual' care to which it is being compared. This has presented dilemmas in international research when studies have been carried out in countries with differing 'usual' standards of care compared with other participating countries or the country funding the research.

In research among vulnerable groups, particular attention must be paid to any risks, including those that may be viewed as relatively harmless. This is especially important when individuals may not be able to articulate concerns themselves.

Rights-based approach (dignity of the research participant)

Individual freedoms and recognised 'rights' of an individual within a given society are the focus of a rights-based approach. Therefore, the main concern is to establish and respect the views and feelings of prospective research participants. The rights of an individual to refuse participation in any research study must take precedence over any consideration of the wider public good. Value is afforded to the integrity, privacy, safety and human rights of the individual participant. In terms of confidentiality, there is a legal duty to keep patient information confidential and data should be secured against unauthorised access. Particular care should be taken in international collaborations where there are differing values and cultural norms; researchers must not dominate the relationship with research participants, and research participants must: (i) understand the nature and purpose of the research; (ii) have the opportunity to have their questions answered; (iii) give truly informed consent; and (iv) be able to make uncoerced decisions to participate (Benatar, 2002) (see Box 3.4).

Box 3.4 Questions to ask yourself from a rights-based perspective

- Will the research participant's consent be sought and how?
- How is consent dealt with in covert research?
- Are the participants being paid for their involvement?
- At what level may payment be considered coercive?
- Will the individual participant's dignity be protected?
- Will confidentiality be respected and assured by the researcher?
- What precautions are taken to safeguard all data collected?

Research involving competent research participants should only be conducted with their knowledge and consent. Researchers have an obligation to seek consent from all competent people. An individual's refusal to participate should always be respected. Once consent is given it is not necessarily enduring; individuals can withdraw from the study at any time. Consent must be maintained during long-term studies and reviewed if study procedures are altered (Choudhury and Knapp, 2006).

A number of challenges arise where consent cannot be provided by participants themselves and careful consideration must be given to the special legal issues relating to these cases. For example, in the UK, special procedures have to be followed if the proposed research involves the use of information from which NHS patients could be identified, but it is not possible to obtain their informed consent (NRES, 2007).

Combining these three approaches, Foster (2001) provides a framework for ethical review of research. A rights-based judgement is difficult when one cannot be certain of the wishes of an individual research participant; the duty-based approach could on balance regard the research as ethical if it was therapeutic and there was equipoise; a solely goals-based stance would view the research as ethical if it could be shown that ultimately more people would benefit than suffer.

The Foster framework will not necessarily result in any solution regarding the ethical acceptability of a study. In particular, in international studies, researchers should not anticipate a single best set of answers to the questions posed. Responses to individual questions may differ according to the research centre or setting. A judgement concerning the ethical acceptability of the research is made on balancing the risks and benefits of the project being undertaken.

Informed consent

Consent sets the limits for what the researcher can do with research participants or personal data (Simonsen and Nylenna, 2006). Informed consent has been defined as potential participants receiving information necessary to make an informed choice about participation in a study, understanding the information and making a voluntary decision regarding whether to participate (CIOMS, 2002).

Participants must receive *sufficient* information for their consent to be viewed as informed. Achieving informed consent is dependent on the researcher's ability to communicate, and the research participant's sense of freedom to choose. However, it must be acknowledged that there may be difficulties attaining full comprehension in any setting, and that this may be more challenging across diverse international collaborations. For research being undertaken in a variety of locations, additional steps may include community level consultation and permission prior to seeking individual consent. Where the majority of potential participants cannot read or write (so signing consent forms cannot be expected), alternative methods of documenting the individual informed consent process should be adopted, e.g. a record of verbal consent through audio/video tape, or where the researcher signs a form stating that appropriate information was given and verbal consent received, which could be observed by an independent witness (Molyneux *et al.*, 2004; Choudhury and Knapp, 2006).

A study by Rivera *et al.* (2007) examined the level of detail that should be provided to potential research participants balanced against the participants' needs for information and capabilities to understand it. This research was undertaken with three independent groups of researchers based in Africa, Europe and North America. They found that researchers with different types of research backgrounds, from a variety of professional backgrounds, who held different cultural perceptions of informed consent, demonstrated low agreement on what should be included. The top priority was that potential study subjects should receive sufficient information about possible benefits of participating in a study and how it will be conducted. Consensus was achieved regarding the issue of publicising the names of community advisory board members or community representatives. Crucially, they also concluded that the amount of detail provided in the informed consent process should not be excessively comprehensive and information overload may actually hinder understanding.

Regardless of whether the consent form is presented in English, or in a translation, it can be meaningless unless it is explained by someone who fully understands the culture and concerns of the people for whom it is intended (McCabe *et al.*, 2005). Consent forms may require translation. As for other study documentation, forward and back translation methods can be adopted. Independent of the translators, further review may be required by language experts, disease/topic experts and study personnel to discuss any issues that may have arisen during the translation process and piloting of the translated documents. Sufficient time must be allowed both by the researchers and funding agencies to develop comprehensible material (McCabe *et al.*, 2005). For further information regarding the translation of research documentation see Chapter 4.

A number of considerations for adapting the informed consent process to cross-cultural settings have been identified (Robison, 1998; Molyneux *et al.*, 2004; McCabe *et al.*, 2005):

- Minimise legal and scientific jargon in the consent form.
- Consider the sequence of information presented in the consent form to facilitate logical translations into complex languages.
- Allow for community members' review and critique of forms.
- Identify conceptual and linguistic barriers to communicating effectively about research.
- Ensure that those administering consent forms are culturally competent to address questions and potential misunderstandings as the concept of research may be alien.
- Be aware of power relationship between the research team and the community which can impact on the informed consent process.
- The concept of the signed informed consent form may have additional issues regarding confidentiality, anonymity and the act of signing.
- Consider the local setting, for example if telephone support has been offered as a means of communication, offer alternatives for people without telephones.

The concept of informed consent may not translate culturally to all countries as individual rights and the patient–provider relationship can take on different meanings in different locations (Geller *et al.*, 2004). The autonomy of research participants will be influenced by the values held within their population. Researchers undertaking research in countries other than their own must be aware of, and respect, local customs and culture. For example, in some cultural environments, it may be customary to seek advice or permission from a spouse or head of household. In other settings, investigators may need to consult with local community leaders or elders before implementing a study. Notably, the spouse/head of household/community consent is supplementary and not a replacement for individual consent. Therefore this does not necessarily diminish the individual's ability to make his or her own choices, but approaches should be considered so that it is possible to obtain an individual's informed consent and preserve cultural norms and the spirit of the community. This approach may present its own difficulties, for example, it may be unclear who represents a community, conflict may arise when more than one individual/group represents the community's interests and/or community and individual interests may conflict (Geller *et al.*, 2004; Marshall, 2005; Salako, 2006; Choudhury and Knapp, 2006).

The understanding and operation of informed consent procedures are not universal. Consent procedures may be alien to some groups, for example, the requirement of a signature may be interpreted as a legal obligation to participate. Barata *et al.* (2006) studied the perceptions of different minority groups (Portuguese Canadian and Caribbean Canadian immigrants) in understanding the informed consent process. Both participant groups identified the need for information. Consent letters were viewed as providing valuable information that participants used in their decision making process and actually encouraged participation. Verbal explanation of the study allowed participants to ask more questions. Researchers also found that establishing trust was culturally bound and that a fear of exploitation and mistrust was sometimes apparent. Where trust was present, it was associated with the view that the research was legitimate and safe.

This study highlighted the fact that different ethnic groups have different concerns which may require slightly different approaches to recruitment and methods to obtain informed consent. For example, Barata *et al.* (2006) recommended that recruitment and informed consent procedures may be enhanced if facilitated through a trusted community member. Providing study results to participants and other community members may help to demonstrate the benefits of health research, which was an important factor for prospective participants when deciding whether or not to take part. Viewing informed consent as a process rather than as a discrete event that ends with the signing of the consent form, could enhance the opportunities of the research team to promote trust between participants and researchers, before, during and after the study is complete.

Researchers need to respect the limits of participants' understanding and capacity to deal with difficult information, allowing time for reflection and questioning. For adults incapable of informed consent and for research involving children, assent should be sought and proxy consent from the legal representative, parent or guardian (Choudhury and Knapp, 2006). Informed consent must be fashioned to meet the needs, culture, and context of the community in which it is being used (Geller *et al.*, 2004).

Summary of ethical considerations for the international researcher

Peer review process

The first step in the ethical review process should be that undertaken by the research team, perhaps aided by senior research colleagues, representatives of the potential participants and/or other stakeholders. A framework for review, as discussed above, may be useful for this. Only when ethical issues identified by the team have been addressed should independent review be sought.

Ethical review process

Researchers have the responsibility of complying with the ethical rules of the countries and institutions in which the research is taking place. If this is problematic due to the lack of ethical committees then appropriate alternatives should be identified. Review should be undertaken by individuals who are familiar with the laws, regulations and ethical requirements and expectations of the participating countries as well as having experience of the research process. In some countries, there may be diverse additional national and/or local requirements. Disagreements and resolving conflicts between decisions of committees in different countries can be a challenge. It is important that the scientific integrity of any international research project is not compromised by varying requirements, and adequate communication about these among research team members is crucial.

Protecting and respecting the community and participants

Awareness of, and sensitivity to, the social and cultural perspectives regarding the research objectives and procedures of the participating countries should be demonstrated. In addition, individual participants' autonomy should be respected. Scientific endeavour must not take precedence over the well-being of participants. The investigation should be discontinued if proven harmful. Participants should be volunteers and risks as low as possible, irrespective of potential future benefits.

Providing information to participants and obtaining informed consent

Information including the project's aims, methods, duration of an individual's participation and what it will involve, foreseeable benefits/risks, safeguards for confidentiality, freedom to abstain or withdraw from the study at any time, funding sources and institutional affiliations should be provided to research participants. Information must be conveyed in a way that is both effective and mindful of varying linguistic, social and cultural perspectives of the different population groups. There should be opportunities for potential participants to ask questions. Once the information is understood, then researchers can request participation.

Voluntary informed consent must be obtained, based on the principle that competent individuals are entitled to choose freely whether or not to participate in research. Informed consent protects an individual's freedom of choice and autonomy. Researchers must not deceive or intimidate any participant. Excessive financial inducements to participate may compromise the extent to which decisions of whether or not to participate are genuinely voluntary. The acceptability and impact of offering inducements may also vary between settings and locations, and be influenced by local socio-cultural and economic factors. A distinction can usually be drawn between these payments and reimbursement for inconvenience, expenses incurred or time spent on the project. Any compensation should be approved by the ethics committees.

Conclusion

This chapter has introduced the central concepts of research ethics focusing on issues of concern and relevance in international research. International guidelines have been included to inform researchers of the ethical considerations for research involving human participants, however their application within individual countries does vary. Despite international guidelines, researchers need to allow time for establishing and meeting the requirements of all participating countries. In international collaborations, special consideration must be given to the value systems and cultural norms of local populations regarding the place and operation of the research proposed.

The Foster (2001) approach to ethical review provides one example of some of the issues to reflect upon when preparing an ethically sound research protocol for an international collaboration. It highlights the potential difficulties of balancing the benefits and concerns of different types of research, in order for ethical acceptability to be established. Most importantly, for all research involving human participants, a theoretically and methodically sound research design is required and voluntary informed consent must be obtained.

References

Barata P C, Gucciardi E, Ahmad F, Stewart D E (2006). Cross-cultural perspectives on research participation and informed consent. *Social Sci Med* 62: 479–490.

Benatar S R (2002). Reflections and recommendations on research ethics in developing countries. *Social Sci Med* 54: 1131–1141.

Choudhury S R, Knapp L A (2006). A review of international and UK-based ethical guidelines for researchers conducting nontherapeutic genetic studies in developing countries. *Eur J Hum Genet* 14: 9–16.

CIOMS (Council for International Organizations of Medical Sciences) (2002). *International Ethical Guidelines for Biomedical Research Involving Human Subjects*. Geneva, Switzerland: Council for International Organizations for Medical Sciences.

Dresden E, McElmurry B J, McCreary L L (2003). Approaching ethical reasoning in nursing research through a communitarian perspective. *J Prof Nurs* 19: 295–304.

Foster C (ed.) (1996). *Manual for Research Ethics Committees*, 4th edn. London: King's College University of London.

Foster C (2001). *The Ethics of Medical Research on Humans*. Cambridge: Cambridge University Press.

Geller S E, Patel A, Niak V A, Goudar S S, Edlavitch S A, Kodkany B S, Derman R J (2004). Conducting international collaborative research in developing nations. *Int J Gynecol Obstet* 87: 267–271.

Hearnshaw H (2004). Comparison of requirements of research ethics committees in 11 European countries for a non-invasive interventional study. *BMJ* 328: 140–141.

Kennedy H P, Renfrew M J, Madi B C, Opoku D, Thompson J B (2006). The conduct of ethical research collaboration across international and culturally diverse communities. *Midwifery* 22: 100–107.

Marshall P A (2005). Human rights, cultural pluralism, and international health research. *Theor Med Bioeth* 26: 529–557.

McCabe M, Morgan F, Curley H, Begay R, Gohdes D M (2005). The informed consent process in a cross-cultural setting: is the process achieving the intended result? *Ethn Dis* 15: 300–304.

Molyneux C S, Peshu N, Marsh K. (2004). Understanding of informed consent in a low-income setting: three case studies from the Kenyan coast. *Soc Sci Med* 59: 2547–2559.

NRES (National Patient Safety Agency and National Research Ethics Service) (2007). Facilitating and promoting ethical research. http://www.nres.npsa. nhs.uk/ (accessed 19 December 2007).

Olsen D P (on behalf of Working Group for the Study of Ethical Issues in International Nursing Research) (2003). Ethical considerations in international nursing research: a report from the International Centre for Nursing Ethics. *Nurs Ethics* 10: 122–137.

Rashad A M, Phipps F M, Haith-Cooper M (2004). Obtaining informed consent in an Egyptian research study. *Nurs Ethics* 11: 394–399.

Rivera R, Borasky D, Rice R, Carayon F, Wong E. (2007). Informed consent: an international researchers' perspective. *Am J Public Health* 97: 25–30.

Robison V A (1998). Some ethical issues in international collaborative research in developing countries. *Int Dent J* 48: 552–556.

Salako S E (2006). The Declaration of Helsinki 2000: ethical principles and the dignity of difference. *Med Law* 25: 341–354.

Schüklenk U (2005). Module one: introduction to research ethics. *Dev World Bioeth* 5: 1–13.

Simonsen S, Nylenna M (2006). Basic ethical, professional and legal principles of biomedical research. *Scand J Work Environ Health Suppl* 2: 5–14.

Wagner R M (2003). Ethical review of research involving human subjects: when and why is IRB review necessary? *Muscle Nerve* 28: 27–39.

World Health Organization website: www.who.int (accessed 19 December 2007).

4

Instrument development and validation

The focus of this chapter is instrument development and validation, with emphasis on the additional considerations in international collaborations. It begins with a brief discussion of different methodological approaches (quantitative, qualitative or a combination) that may be employed and the types of research question for which they are most appropriate. The chapter then addresses the principles and concepts of instrument development and validation within these quantitative and qualitative paradigms, before discussing the application of these principles and concepts in the context of international studies. The extra dimension of international research presents additional challenges. Here, instruments need to be relevant, applicable and valid not only in a number of countries, but also in different cultural and healthcare (policy) systems, and possibly different languages.

Setting clear research aims and objectives

As with any local or national project, be it big or small, a crucial part of the research process is the development of a set of clearly stated aims and objectives. It is imperative to have a coherent understanding of the specific research questions, so that the methodological approach and instruments can be designed in such a way that they elicit relevant and usable information. This will also involve a comprehensive review of the relevant international literature to establish and build upon what is already known, and to refine the aim and objectives of the international project accordingly (see Chapter 2).

As this chapter focuses on instrument development and validation for use across international boundaries, it is important in this context to articulate research objectives that clearly identify the aim of the international collaboration. For example, is the main aim of the collaboration to establish a research network, which will result in expertise informed by different cultures, healthcare systems, languages, etc., where individual projects may remain national? Or is the aim of the international collaboration to undertake research that is relevant and possible at an international level, so that the data collected allow cross-country comparisons? The latter option will require a focus on issues of significance across national (and health system) boundaries. Here, the relevance across countries needs to take precedence over issues that may only be important in one or two countries. In other words, the international research partners need to decide on whether the level of analysis will be national or international, and whether the unit of analysis will be individuals or groups. As the latter is probably the more complex approach, and is indeed the focus of this chapter and book, the following sections will concentrate on research design and instrument development for the purpose of cross-country relevance, application, analysis, comparison and interpretation.

Research questions – What is being measured and how?

Once the aim of the international collaboration has been clearly agreed – in the form of explicitly reported aims and objectives or research questions – the next step should already emerge. This is about determining the best way to answer the research questions, the *how*.

First, the research questions will guide whether the most appropriate methodologies are likely to be quantitative or qualitative, or indeed a combination. This, in turn, will depend on whether the main purpose of the study is explorative, descriptive (including measuring), explanatory or experimental (e.g. evaluating an intervention or hypothesis testing). Exploration is undertaken when little is known about the subject and researchers are beginning to familiarise themselves with the topic. Descriptive studies characterise situations, events, beliefs, etc. to answer questions such as what, where, when and how. Studies in which the goal is explanation are designed to answer questions of why. Experimental studies are usually undertaken using a structured quantitative approach and some form of experimental design. The following sections provide an overview of the principles of quantitative and qualitative methodologies that are relevant to instrument development, before turning to more issues and procedures within each of these methodological paradigms that arise in the context of international studies: in particular, language and translation; and cross-cultural equivalence.

Quantitative approaches

Surveys are probably the most commonly used method in health services and medicines-related research, and they can be used for exploratory, descriptive or explanatory purposes. Undertaking a survey usually means that a relatively large sample of people are selected from a pre-determined population (for a discussion of sampling see Chapter 5), and a set of highly structured data are then collected from those individuals. These data may serve to describe populations (following carefully selected samples) and measure events, behaviours or attitudes. Statistical analyses aim to establish links and relationships between variables/attributes/characteristics and make some inferences about the wider population. This provides 'snap-shot' data, either at just one point in time (cross-sectional survey) or at two or more points in time (longitudinal surveys).

In order to enable quantification and statistical analysis, data need to be collected in a standardised and structured form. In survey research, data may be collected by means of a self-administered questionnaire, or a structured face-to-face or telephone interview. The questionnaire or interview schedule, developed for this purpose, comprises the research instrument or tool. The instrument or tool, when applied to a population of interest, must be known to provide an accurate reflection of the issues or phenomena under study. This attribute of a research instrument is referred to as its validity. For many commonly measured demographic and health attributes, validated tools (commonly batteries of questions) already exist. If this is the case it is advisable to use such tools, rather than designing and validating new ones, as this will save time, avoid duplication and allow comparison with other studies that have used the same instrument.

The Question Bank (QB) is an extremely valuable resource as it contains original questionnaires for many UK national, and also some European, social and health surveys (ESRC, 2007). It also contains details on these questionnaires and more general documentation to support the reasoning behind, and conceptual approach to, measuring certain issues, such as quality of life. In its mission statement the QB states that 'the website has been designed to help users locate examples of specific research questions and see them in the context within which they have been used for data collection. It is intended to assist with the design of new survey questionnaires ... and the teaching of survey research methods' (ESRC, 2007). Even though the QB has a UK focus, similar national surveys exist in many other countries (Hupkens *et al.*,

1999) and similar websites may be available too. The MAPI Research Institute (www.mapi-research.fr) may prove to be a valuable resource. This is an 'international company with a special interest in advancing the worldwide use of patient-reported and clinical assessments through linguistic validation for appropriate cross-cultural use and interpretation.'

A huge number of research instruments have been developed to measure a wide range of constructs, phenomena and attributes (e.g. quality of life, health beliefs, attitudes, experiences, etc.) in various population groups in countries around the world. A literature search may uncover many potential measures that might be adapted for, or incorporated into, a study. Some of these may be well-established tools or instruments which have been extensively tested for their validity and reliability across different populations and settings. For others, these features may be less well assured. Before selecting any tool, it will be important to make an independent assessment of its likely validity and reliability when applied among particular population groups, situations and settings. Thus, researchers need to give significant thought to the choice of standardised instrument, taking into consideration its conceptual model, its characteristics such as its administration and scoring methods, and its psychometric properties (see Francis, 2001 for a more detailed discussion).

In her personal account, Dana Darwish describes issues that arose in the development of guidelines for the management of cardiovascular disease for patients in Jordan (Personal account 4.1). The starting point was internationally accepted guidelines, which largely emanated from research in the US, the UK and other parts of the developed world. She discusses problems that arose and how she addressed them to achieve a tool that was acceptable, feasible and effective in the context of healthcare in the Jordanian setting.

Questionnaire instrument/item development

In those instances where a validated instrument is unavailable, a new instrument will need to be developed. A questionnaire contains a number of individual items which generally consist of two elements: the question (or statement) on the one hand and the possible answer categories or response options on the other (Babbie, 2007). The construction of both is important for the design of a valid and reliable tool, and following a brief discussion of types of questions and statements that may be used, the terms used to describe and measure

PERSONAL ACCOUNT 4.1

DANA DARWISH

Adapting drug utilisation guidelines for patients with cardiovascular disease in diverse countries and settings

This was a multi-stage project with the overall aim of evaluating the use of cardiovascular drugs in Jordanian hospitals, and to propose areas for therapy optimisation (Darwish *et al.*, 2001). The project involved the development of a tool for the assessment of cardiovascular drug use in three different health settings in Jordan: the university, the government and the private hospital settings.

The tool was developed based on international cardiology guidelines largely emanating from the USA, the UK and other European and developed countries. This was then adapted and validated for the use in Jordanian settings in terms of the acceptability, feasibility and effectiveness of their application.

Successful transfer of guidelines requires their adaptation to the new setting's needs and limitations. For instance, to take into consideration the variability in resources and drug availability across the different settings, such as developed versus developing countries, or private versus public sectors. While most drugs are available in the developed world, many settings in the less-developed countries are struggling with limited resources and drug shortages. While all patients and professionals aspire to high standards of care, if such limitations are not taken into account the guidelines (instrument) could be unworkable.

It is also important to understand the study settings' characteristics, e.g. perceptions on the use of guidelines, factors that influence medical practice, drug information sources commonly used, as it would pave the way to effectively design and implement guidelines.

To ensure *feasibility/applicability* of the developed guidelines, it is recommended to:

- Conduct a preliminary exploration to establish the need for the guidelines and highlight the benefits, which would occur from their implementation, particularly to decision-makers in the study setting.
- Have the developed guidelines reviewed by a panel of local experts to assess their feasibility.
- Conduct preliminary field testing of the guidelines for further tuning.
- Address the need for translation (if applicable) and the associated issues of content validity.

continued overleaf

Personal account 4.1 (continued)

To ensure *acceptability* of the guidelines it is necessary to:

- Get opinion leaders and key practitioners involved in the project, as it would establish support for the project and endorse its findings to other practitioners.
- Agree with the participants on the sources and methods used for developing the guidelines.
- Establish consensus on the recommendations included in the local guidelines and clearly justify any deviations from international guidelines.

To ensure *effectiveness*:

- The effectiveness of the developed guidelines in assessing clinical practice was verified by submitting a subset of cases (10–20%) to a panel of senior cardiologists to assess the outcome of practice evaluation.

Reference

Darwish D, Dhillon S, Smith F, Al-Khawad A (2001). Evaluation of drug use in cardiac diseases at Jordanian hospitals. *Proceedings of the 5th Congress of the Association of Colleges of Pharmacy in the Arab World.* Amman, Jordan.

---

instrument 'quality' will be explained. It is also worth noting that processes of item development and validation will be very similar for surveys conducted with the use of a telephone or face-to-face interview schedule. The main difference is that with self-administered question-naires, respondents see the questions written down in front of them and respond to them themselves. In interviews, on the other hand, an inter-viewer takes on the role of asking questions or presenting other types of items, such as attitude statements, as well as recording responses (see Chapter 6).

Many items in questionnaires will be questions. In line with the aim of collecting highly structured data to meet pre-determined study objectives, these will mostly be closed, i.e. providing respondents with a list of possible answers. The simplest of these are those giving only 'yes' and 'no' options. However, a number of other techniques may be employed such as allowing multiple responses or asking respondents to rank responses according to their importance. Opinions or attitudes are often measured by presenting a number of statements to which respon-dents are asked to agree or disagree, commonly on a five-point Likert scale.

There are many rules that need to be observed when designing both a questionnaire and the individual items. For example, questions (and statements), need to be clear and not open to differing interpretations, relevant, not leading or value-laden and unbiased. Negative items are best avoided as they are more likely to be misread. Questions must possess content, construct and/or criterion validity. The questionnaire should be attractive and easy to follow. General principles of questionnaire design are discussed in many texts (Oppenheim, 1992; Smith, 2005; Babbie, 2007).

Instrument quality: reliability and validity

The data obtained through the use of a questionnaire (or indeed any methodology) can only be as good as the tool used to collect these data. Terms that may be used to understand and define 'quality' are 'validity' and 'reliability.' 'Reliability' is concerned with whether the repeated use or application of the same instrument or questions yields consistent data. This is an important concept, but one that should not be confused with accuracy. For example, an instrument may gather similar responses on each application, however if the responses do not reflect what is true and/or meaningful then that particular instrument would be inappropriate for use in that set of circumstances.

The concept of 'validity' is defined as the extent to which an instrument (or rather the individual questions and items within it) measures what it is supposed to measure. Ensuring validity is crucially important in survey research, and generally involves testing the instrument in a small sample from the population in which it is to be used (pilot). There are different types of validity, which are briefly defined here, but the reader is referred to other textbooks for more detailed definitions, examples, and how to test them (Smith, 2002; Babbie, 2007).

Face validity refers to the apparent likelihood that an item or tool will provide an accurate representation of the phenomena of interest. That is 'prima facia', or without further testing or investigation, the instrument appears to be intuitively asking the right questions and presenting relevant response categories. Checking for face validity aims to identify relatively obvious problems with the measure, and is often established by asking colleagues and/or different stakeholders for comments. There are three further types of validity: content, construct and criterion validity. *Content validity* is concerned with the extent to which a measure covers the range of issues or meanings included within a concept. An assessment of content validity must be made for the instrument (e.g. questionnaire) as a whole as well as for each question/item with its responses. For individual questions, the possible responses must include all the options that respondents may feel are relevant and important to them. Only then can a particular question accurately reflect the true range of the respondents' experiences and/or views. Content validity is usually addressed early on in instrument development. Besides a detailed review of the relevant literature, it may involve a preliminary qualitative study which helps to identify the range and detail of relevant issues. *Construct validity* is based on the underlying relationship among variables and is concerned with whether, and how well, item(s) relate to a construct or concept. Finally, *criterion validity*, sometimes called 'predictive validity', refers to how well the instrument corresponds to other measures of the same variable, or an external criterion.

Developing quantitative tools for international research

After the previous section briefly highlighted general issues relating to the development of a survey instrument, this section deals with the specific and additional aspects that need to be observed when designing an instrument that is to be used in an international study. This brings with it a whole new, and very important, set of issues to ensure that the questionnaire is relevant and comprehensible to people in a number of different countries. Furthermore, in order to allow cross-country comparisons, each individual item, and the instrument as a whole, needs to have the *same* meaning in each country, i.e. measure the same issue or concept.

The fact that each country will have a different healthcare system, and within this different rules, regulations and practices, may mean that not all concepts can be measured and compared across different countries and systems. To allow comparison it is therefore important to identify the issues that are relevant in all countries. The detail and depth of data gathering, where the issues and specific policies under investigation are country-specific, may be best explored at a national level. The main aim, and particular strength, of conducting international research will be to accomplish cross-national relevance and comparability.

Administering questionnaires in a number of countries where different languages are spoken with the purpose of cross-country comparison means that these instruments need to measure the same concepts or items in each country and in each language. They need to achieve cultural and functional equivalence. 'Cultural equivalence' refers to similar meaning and relevance of constructs being examined across cultures (Jones *et al.*, 2001). 'Functional equivalence' refers to the 'degree to which a concept performs in the same way or elicits similar responses from individuals in two or more cultures' (Jones *et al.*, 2001), and Jones *et al.* provide good examples to help understand these principles.

Instrument translation and cultural equivalence

Simply translating an existing research instrument is inadequate to produce a robust tool for research across different countries and may result in conceptually dissimilar instruments. It is essential that for any research study, differences in the findings between locations are demonstrably due to true differences in the concept being measured and not because of inadequacies in the instrument which may be a consequence of cultural and linguistic differences. A number of models of *equivalence* are evident on reviewing existing cross-cultural research, e.g. conceptual, item, semantic, operational, measurement and functional equivalence (Behling and Law, 2000). Bowden and Fox-Rushby (2003) provide an in-depth discussion of these definitions in relation to their review of the process of translation and adaptation of generic health-related quality of life measures in Africa, Asia, Eastern Europe, the Middle East and South America.

Many issues require consideration when translating existing instruments (Behling and Law, 2000; Jones *et al.*, 2001; Abbott *et al.*, 2001; Yu *et al.*, 2004; Willgerodt *et al.*, 2005; Wang *et al.*, 2006):

- Certain concepts present linguistic and conceptual challenges
- It may be difficult to find qualified bilingual translators
- Bilingual translators can bring to the setting language mannerisms and concepts that belong to the source language culture; this can present problems to the typically monolingual respondents of the translated instrument
- The backgrounds of the forward- and back-translators in terms of education/socio-economics must be shared with that of the target population
- Literal translation can result in grammatically awkward translated versions; bilingual translators may automatically and subconsciously correct for any awkward syntax during the back-translation process because they are able to distinguish the intent of the original question
- In producing the target instrument, problems can arise if grammatical nuances of the source language are retained

- It may be necessary to develop versions that are clearly understood by respondents who speak different dialects or have different levels of education
- Certain expressions do not exist in other languages; some words/phrases are impossible to translate meaningfully; some issues are not important in other cultures.

The translation methods adopted and the processes used to examine equivalence must be clearly documented to avoid problems relating to grammatical translation, cultural usage and experience, syntax and concept interpretation (Wang et al., 2006).

Brislin's translation–back-translation model

One of the most common approaches to translating an existing validated tool is Brislin's translation–back-translation method (Brislin, 1970). This involves an iterative process in which one bilingual translator translates (from source to target language) and another bilingual back-translates (from target to source language) blindly (i.e. with no knowledge of the source questionnaire). Ideally, these translators should be familiar with the broad content (area of interest) of the source questionnaire. The resulting translations are then reviewed by a number of 'raters', and pre-testing of the translated instruments may occur. This will result in an agreement on changes to the target, and possibly source, questionnaire, avoiding errors that lead to differences in meaning. If errors are found, Brislin recommends repeating translation and back-translation. This is a potentially time-consuming and costly approach, as each repetition requires new bilingual translators. Therefore, many researchers use variations and adaptations of Brislin's model (Jones et al., 2001; Cha et al., 2007), where group discussions among the bilinguals involved in translations and back-translations aim to establish instruments with cultural equivalence. These approaches of reaching consensus can also include the project steering committee or advisory group, who will be familiar with the instrument and its purpose, as well as the researchers themselves.

In her personal account, Ellen Schafheutle highlights a range of issues that emerged during the process of translation and back-translation of a research instrument for use in six countries (Personal account 4.2). These issues extended beyond cultural equivalence and meaning but all had to be addressed if data collection was to be successful.

PERSONAL ACCOUNT 4.2

ELLEN SCHAFHEUTLE

Patient survey questionnaire development and validation in six countries

Following the results obtained in patient (and also physician) focus groups in six European countries (see Personal account 6.1), we designed a patient questionnaire for use in all six countries, with the ultimate aim of being able to analyse and compare across the different countries and systems (Schafheutle *et al.*, 2000, 2004; Atella *et al.*, 2005). Questionnaire development and validation took place in a number of stages, starting with a list of issues that ought to be covered, through to a final questionnaire that existed in five different languages. This involved several meetings in Brussels, teleconferences and e-mail correspondence, where good communication, the clear setting of leadership, roles and responsibilities of the different partners, deadlines for actions, timely responses and agreement among partners all proved vitally important. Despite the importance of these issues, they were commonly not achieved fully, thus hindering the effective progress of questionnaire development.

Questionnaire development was co-ordinated by the UK team ('reinforced action'), who initiated the process by composing a first draft questionnaire for discussion at one of our ENDEP meetings in Brussels. This draft underwent several cycles of additions and amendments following discussions – at meetings and through other forms of communication – which ensured that:

- All items that needed to be covered to achieve the objectives were indeed included. (We did this by compiling a document listing the rationale for each question or battery.)
- The items used validated tools where available (e.g. health status, UK income) and, based on a literature review and the focus groups findings, developed items were short, simple, clear, unambiguous and avoiding colloquialisms.
- All items were relevant in all countries. (For example, in a battery presenting strategies patients may use to cope with the cost of prescribed medicines, an item exploring the use of pre-payment certificates had to be removed, because similar arrangements did not exist in the other countries.)

Once the final version of the source questionnaire had been agreed in English, this needed to be translated into four other languages, ensuring cultural and content equivalence in six different countries, healthcare and medication co-payment systems. For this purpose we used a combination of elements contained in Brislin's well-recognised model of back-translation (Brislin, 1970), thus accommodating time and cost constraints of several cycles of iterative back-translations, requiring several bilingual translators for

continued overleaf

Personal account 4.2 (continued)

each language. Each ENDEP partner (I believe) translated the source questionnaire into their individual language. They then employed a bilingual person with insight into the subject matter but no knowledge of the actual questionnaire to translate this back into English. I then reviewed and compared the source and the back-translated questionnaires. As I am bilingual and a native German speaker, I also reviewed the German and Austrian questionnaire translations. I identified any discrepancies and also issued clarification where necessary. This process showed that discrepancies were due to a much wider range of reasons than just translation and cultural equivalence. Those issues that were of a translation nature were often more far reaching than anticipated, demonstrating that the majority of partners and other people that helped with the translation were not actually professional translators, nor indeed had a level of understanding of both languages that was truly bilingual.

However, there were numerous non-translation issues which were commonly about accuracy. This meant that my checking went far beyond that of checking meaning following translation, but ensured accuracy of transfer, e.g. that all countries used the same type and number of battery questions, that answer categories matched and used identical coding etc. It showed the vital importance of such checking to ensure that the different questionnaires were collecting the same information in the same way, just in different languages. The table below lists some of the issues that were identified and resolved following discussion and agreement, and demonstrates how crucial such a checking process is.

Issues that were identified in the process of translation and back-translation: much more than just cultural equivalence and 'meaning'

Source language (English)	Following translation and back-translation
Equivalence of meaning	
'Eye or ear problems'	'Eye or ear infections'
'How many times have you been to see a doctor on your own behalf in the last three months?'	'Over the past three months, how many times have you taken the initiative to visit a doctor?'
'I ask pharmacy staff to recommend what medicine to buy.'	'I ask the pharmacist to recommend what medicine to buy.' (similar make-up of pharmacy staff and their duties/responsibilities in country in question)
'I ask the doctor to make the prescribed medicines as cheap as possible.'	'I ask the doctor to consider the prescription charge I have to pay.'

'I ask for the doctor to make the prescribed medicine(s) as cheap as possible.'

'I ask the doctor to prescribe a relatively cheap/reasonably priced medicine.'

'Do you ever feel you have to think about how much money you have available to spend when you obtain medicines (. . .)?'

1. 'Does your economic situation ever have an impact on how you generally buy drugs from the pharmacy?
2. 'Is the amount of money you spend on medicines a financial problem for you?'

'The size/amount of the prescription charge stops me from going to see a doctor.'

'Knowing I will not be able to afford the prescription charge stops me from going to see a doctor.'

Translation wrong as not professional translators and English not at bilingual level

Over-the-counter

Out of pocket

Disability

Injury

'I eat a healthy diet.'

'I diet.'

Accuracy and un-ambiguity of translation

Continuous loss of appetite

Loss of appetite

'I take medicine(s) prescribed by a doctor.'

'I get the doctor to prescribe something for my dyspepsia.'

Medicalisation of lay language

High blood pressure

Hypertension

Hay fever

Seasonal allergic rhinitis

'I take less of my medicine to make it last longer.'

'I decrease my daily dose of medicines in order to make the treatment last longer.'

Accuracy (other than pure translation)

'Thinking back over the last FOUR weeks, have you suffered from any of the conditions below?'

'Thinking back a few weeks, have you suffered from any of the conditions below?'

Instructions to clarify that following battery is about both prescription and over the counter medicines

Lacks instructions to clarify that following battery is about both prescription and over the counter medicines

Accuracy of coding

Answer categories coded 0–4

Answer categories coded 1–5

continued overleaf

Personal account 4.2 (continued)

References

Atella V, Schafheutle E, Noyce P, Hassell K (2005). Affordability of medicines and
patients' cost reduction behaviors: empirical evidence based on SUR estimates
from Italy and the UK. *Appl Health Econ Health Policy* 4: 23–35.
Brislin R W (1970). Back-translation for cross-cultural research. *J Cross-Cultural
Psychol* 1: 185–216.
Schafheutle E I, Hassell K, Noyce P R (2000). Developing an instrument for studying
the impact of patient charge systems for pharmaceuticals on the uptake of
medicines. EUPHA congress Paris (France), 14–16 December 2000,
Conference Proceedings, p. 290.
Schafheutle E I, Hassell K, Noyce P R (2004). Coping with prescription charges in the
UK. *Int J Pharmacy Pract* 12: 239–246.

Cross-cultural equivalence and relevance in different healthcare systems

Using terms such as culture rather than language suggests that the two
are not the same. Different cultures have to do with different histories
and traditions which affect not only the way systems and policies have
developed, but also the way people view them and behave within them.
Indeed, cultural differences can exist in countries where the spoken
language is the same, and some differences exist in the meaning or use
of terms and concepts in just one language.

In countries where more than one official language is spoken, there
may still be a certain level of cultural difference, but nevertheless they
tend to have a common set of healthcare policies, and questionnaires
may need to be administered in all official languages to make sure that
no relevant population group is excluded. Examples of countries where
there are more than one official language are Belgium (French, Flemish
and German); Switzerland (German, French and Italian); Canada
(English and French). In addition there are many countries where significant proportions of the population speak languages other than what is
considered the official language. For example, in some UK studies, translations need to be made available for a whole range of spoken languages
such as Hindi, Urdu, Gujarati, Turkish and Somali. Such an approach
can be essential if questionnaires (and indeed other methodologies or
tools) aim to gather data from a representative sample of a population
with a high proportion of minority groups (for example in inner city
areas in England), or to focus on the experiences, views and needs of
minority groups. In many less-developed countries there may be
numerous local languages in addition to official ones. Literacy may also

be an issue, especially in a situation where a local language is generally employed in its spoken but not a written form.

Sabine Nebel, in Personal account 4.3 regarding a socio-nutritional study in six areas of three Mediterranean regions (southern Italy, south-eastern Spain and Crete), identified a number of challenges with respect to the linguistic and cultural adaptation of the project questionnaire. In particular, she experienced problems associated with illiteracy among the communities participating in the study, as well as these populations speaking local dialects and not the principal language(s) of the country into which the data collection materials had been translated.

PERSONAL ACCOUNT 4.3

SABINE NEBEL

Design and application of a questionnaire about socio-nutritional values in three countries

This report relates to the European Union-funded research project 'Local Food-Nutraceuticals' (LFN), which aimed at contributing to the continued use of traditional wild food plants, as well as to the search for new nutraceuticals from local resources, which are of potential interest in the prevention of age-related diseases (Local Food-Nutraceuticals Consortium, 2005). The LFN project included specialists from several fields such as ethnobotany, pharmacognosy, pharmacology and nutrition from the UK, Germany, Poland, Spain, Italy, Switzerland and Greece.

One part of the LFN project was a socio-nutritional study on the consumption of traditional food plants and its relation to social, economic and anthropological factors in three rural areas of the Mediterranean: in southern Italy, south-eastern Spain and Crete. The questionnaire was developed for household members aged over 18. The first challenge was to design a questionnaire with the different members of the LFN consortium. Several meetings were necessary to draft a first proposal, including all stimuli from the different cultures and backgrounds. A difficult task was to design a questionnaire to be used in all three countries in order to be able to compare the gathered data. While it has been recognised that there is a need for culturally appropriate ways to ask questions in surveys (Edwards *et al.*, 2005), little has been written about using questionnaires themselves in different cultural contexts.

The outcome of the study was very positive, and only some minor changes had to be adopted in each country. Interestingly, one specific question regarding factors influencing the choice of food products (e.g. 'to maintain a healthy diet', 'cost' or 'taste'), where the participants had to rate factors as

continued overleaf

Personal account 4.3 (continued)

'not important', 'sometimes important' or 'very important', produced different reactions from the participants in different countries. Participants in southern Italy and south-eastern Spain did not understand clearly how and why they had to rate the different factors, while in Greece the participants did not report any problems in understanding the process.

In general, the outcome of the study was a very positive experience from designing, conducting and analysing the questionnaire within the LFN consortium.

A number of challenges were faced during this project relating to the following factors:

- This was interdisciplinary research with a large project team.
- It was necessary to design a tool to be used in several countries.
- The questionnaire was designed in an urban context but used in a rural context.
- The illiteracy of older household members in rural areas of the Mediterranean was underestimated.
- Language issues included the problem that the questionnaire, information leaflets and consent forms used in the study were translated into the principal (national) languages of each of the study sites (Italian, Spanish, Greek), but the main target population only spoke a local dialect and not the national language.
- The socio-nutritional study was conducted by different members of the LFN consortium.
- Methodological problems included the length of interview for participants of the study.

References

Edwards S, Nebel S, Heinrich M (2005). Questionnaire surveys: methodological and epistemological problems for field-based ethnopharmacologists. *J Ethnopharmacol* 100; 30–36.

Local Food-Nutraceuticals Consortium (2005) Understanding local Mediterranean diets: A multidisciplinary pharmacological and ethnobotanical approach. *Pharmacol Res* 52: 353–366.

Translating instruments is a significant challenge and requires adequate time and resources to achieve an equivalent tool in the target language and culture. Ideally, the goal of this aspect of any international research work is to achieve an instrument that is equivalent in terms of semantics and content by undertaking a robust translation process followed by pilot testing to determine translation accuracy and the psychometric properties of the new instrument.

Table 4.1 Language adaptations required for specific wording in a questionnaire used in two English-speaking countries

USA	UK
Medications	Medicines
Pills	Tablets
Refill	Repeat prescription (dispensed)
Emergency room	Accident & emergency department
Healthful	Healthy

Even when translation is not required, a questionnaire that is developed for, and administered in, a number of English-speaking countries (such as the UK, USA, Canada, Australia and New Zealand) would still need to be checked and adapted for cultural and functional equivalence. This also applies when using existing validated instruments that have been developed in a country other than the one in which they are to be used. As an example to illustrate this, Table 4.1 lists some examples of words and phrases that were 'anglicised' from the US context into a UK one.

Nevertheless, some of the existing, validated measures, despite being highly sophisticated, may not be (easily) transferable into another country and culture. The way certain concepts are measured in a particular country will be embedded in its history and culture. Cultural norms, for example, impose on social classification, and it may be difficult to transfer a system derived in one country to others (National Statistics, 2007). Indeed, the importance will be in the equivalence of the concept, and the attributes through which this is defined, in the participating countries.

In their personal account, comparing perceptions about medicines and illness between Portugal and the UK, Filipa Costa and colleagues illustrate the influence of culturally defined issues such as literacy and religion, in affecting responses to a questionnaire (Personal account 4.4).

Qualitative approaches

Definitions and relevant methods

Qualitative (field) research is a method of naturalistic enquiry, aiming to study people in their everyday social settings and thus collect naturally occurring data (Bowling, 2002). Generally, it describes phenomena in words rather than numbers, and is employed to address questions of

PERSONAL ACCOUNT 4.4

FILIPA A COSTA, CATHERINE DUGGAN AND IAN BATES

Comparing perceptions about medicines and illness in two countries: how religion and education may impact on validity and reliability of adapted survey tools

There is, for non-English speaking countries, a demand for measurement tools validated in their own language. The adaptation of scales is important when developing interventions to improve patient care. When undertaking projects across international boundaries, researchers must have a deep understanding of the cultural issues embedded in each country involved.

A study aiming to adapt a survey tool to measure patients' desires for information, perceptions about medicines and illness was developed (Costa *et al.*, 2007). The survey was adapted using a multi-method approach comprising translation and back-translation, rating of equivalence, and assessment of understanding in various stages of revision involving health professionals and lay input. The tool was tested in a patient sample from different care settings in Portugal and in the UK, and responses were used to explore validity and reliability. Literacy and religion emerged as two potentially discriminating constructs.

Literacy

Although Portuguese literacy problems have reduced in past years, the proportion of the population who are illiterate remains high, especially among the elderly. The instrument included a scale to measure 'the extent of information desired' by respondents. Internal consistency between the items on the scale (measured using Cronbach's alpha) for this scale was $\alpha = 0.607$ in the Portuguese group, compared with 0.73 in the UK (>0.7 is commonly taken as indicating an acceptable value). It was believed that this finding might relate to the low literacy levels characterising inland Portugal because:

- the item 'I read as much as possible about my medicines/illness' was answered differently by illiterate patients, and scores to this scale correlated with educational level;
- lay people considered that the term 'look for' instead of 'reading' should address illiteracy issues, acknowledging they are not the experts: 'Knowledge, is not very simple, for people that cannot read' (patient 3);
- Portuguese patients desired significantly more information than UK patients; interviewees suggested there might be distinct care patterns and Portuguese carers tended to inform patients less about their medication.

Religion

The rating process suggested the item 'I just want to blame someone for the way I feel' required revision, which resulted in a change in this scale's Cronbach's α from 0.081 to 0.665. In a lay panel using vignettes to discuss feelings when diagnosed with a chronic disease, there was a struggle between what is felt and what God allows; with several words classified as 'sinful', albeit with different degrees of severity. Consensus was reached around the least punishable. 'Our Lord had given us that [when found out that they had diabetes], I thanked. We cannot blame God, we must ask Him for health. I accepted because I had to.' [patient 1, F, no education (illiterate), diabetes].

Blame was something they could not do, possibly associated with guilty religious feelings.

Reference

Costa F A, Duggan C, Bates I (2007). A systematic approach to cross-cultural adaptation of survey tools. *Pharm Pract 5*: 115–124.

'how?' and 'why?' Unlike quantitative research, qualitative research is not merely a method of data collection, but is typically a theory-generating activity as well. There are rarely clearly defined hypotheses to be tested, the approach being one of making sense out of an ongoing process that cannot be entirely predicted or anticipated. Analysis therefore is often an iterative process that starts at the beginning of undertaking qualitative research, where early findings feed into further approaches or questions that need to be addressed.

The qualitative methods that are most commonly used in health services and medicines-related research are in-depth (or semi-structured) interviews, focus groups (usually audio-recorded and subsequently transcribed verbatim) and observation. In-depth interviews are one-to-one interviews that allow detailed conversation and exploration of a given topic. Focus groups, on the other hand, are conducted by one (or two) so-called facilitator(s) who oversee a group discussion among between about five and eight (sometimes up to 12) participants. Here, group interaction is the particular strength, and being able to gather information (data) from a number of different individuals in one session. In both approaches, the researcher has a general plan of enquiry rather than a specific set of questions. This allows the researcher to be flexible and responsive to themes emerging during the interview or focus group, an essential element of the qualitative nature of this type of research.

Observation is a qualitative technique which involves the systematic, detailed observation of behaviour and talk, watching and recording what people say and do. It takes place in the natural setting in which (a sample of) the population under investigation lives and/or works. It is particularly valuable when not much is known about the research setting and behaviour within it, and when it is important to see what *actually* happens rather than depend on reports or reflections of respondents obtained in an interview. However, qualitative observation studies tend to be time-consuming and costly.

There are a number of other, less commonly used, methods which often use a combination of quantitative and qualitative approaches to data collection and analysis. These include case studies, consensus methods, such as the Delphi technique, nominal group, Q methodology; action research; diaries; and documentary analysis, where documents (such as government and – local, national and international – policy documents) provide the data sources. Some of these will be discussed further in Chapter 6.

Development of a topic guide

Qualitative interviews and focus groups do not follow a rigid structure of set (often closed) questions as is the case for survey questionnaires, but follow a much looser plan of enquiry, commonly using a so-called 'topic guide' or interview schedule. Such guides can be organised on a continuum ranging from being relatively unstructured, listing a number of topic headings which are broad and employed to encourage the respondents to raise and discuss issues they perceive as relevant, to more semi-structured instruments, where the researcher has a much clearer idea regarding the issues on which respondents' views and comments are being sought. The latter may include some suggestions for prompting, if respondents do not raise particular issues of their own accord.

Data quality: credibility, transferability, dependability, confirmability

As with any research method, each type of qualitative method has its own set of strengths and weaknesses. Some are common across the different types, and are due to the qualitative nature of the research approach, others are more specific to certain methods. The particular strength of all qualitative methods lies in the depth of exploration and understanding they permit, as well as the flexibility, where the approach is responsive and the research design can be modified accordingly. A number of measures may be undertaken to ensure the rigour of qualitative research, and a number of criteria exist that help to assess its quality: credibility, transferability, dependability and confirmability (Robson, 2002). In an international study these must be applied across all settings.

Credibility

Qualitative research has high internal validity as it focuses on the meaning and understanding of a particular concept or issue. In order for qualitative research to be credible, it should be undertaken in such a way that the research topic is accurately identified and described. Triangulation, where different methods of data collection are used to gather evidence concerning the same phenomenon and are used collectively to address the qualitative enquiry, is one method of enhancing credibility. Furthermore, presenting one's findings to respondents or peers can be further approaches to foster credibility.

Transferability

Transferability corresponds to external validity and relates to the generalisability of the study findings (sample) to other settings. As the purpose of qualitative research is the *in-depth* exploration of social phenomena, therefore commonly involving small numbers of individuals and/or settings, statistical generalisation to a population is not an aim. Qualitative research aims for transferability of the findings to a further situation or theory, which is considered suitable to warrant generalisation. The research should be sufficiently detailed that the findings may be examined for transferability in relation to other published work, other settings, or in the formulation of a hypothesis for quantitative exploration.

Dependability

Dependability, analogous to reliability, may be defended through rigorous accounts of the research processes and the presentation of methods of guarding against bias. From the outset, the researcher needs to be honest about the theoretical perspective and any values he or she may hold. The researcher also has to be reflexive about this throughout the whole research process. It is further imperative that qualitative research is conducted in an explicit (transparent) and systematic way (e.g. not ignoring negative or contradictory occurrences), and that sources of error and bias are kept to the minimum (Bowling, 2002).

It is particularly important in qualitative research for the researcher to be reflexive about his or her own role and about potential sources of bias. In this situation the researcher acts as the research instrument, conducting the interviews or moderating the focus group, thus making decisions about pursuing certain issues and not others, or initiating certain prompts, and influencing, to some extent, the way the interview or focus group develops. In observations the fact that the researcher is the research instrument is even more obvious, as he or she decides which occurrences to observe and record. This level of subjectivity continues through to the stage of data analysis, which is commonly addressed by having more than just one researcher draw up, compare and agree the analysis framework, which identifies themes and categories (Smith, 2002). Furthermore, it is good (and common) practice to have more than just one researcher code all, or at least some, of the data independently (i.e. applying the before-mentioned analysis framework), so the consistency of application of the coding frame can be checked (Smith, 2002, 2005). The analysis of qualitative data is covered in more detail in Chapter 6.

Confirmability

Confirmability is the endeavour of objectivity, where the details of the research are examined to determine not only the competency of the research process but also the provision of sufficient information (e.g. research proposal, raw data, coding frames, field notes, analytical notes) to substantiate the relationship between the data and the findings.

Developing qualitative instruments for international research

The previous section presented a brief overview of qualitative research, its methods, the kinds of questions for which it is used, and how to ensure a scientific approach; the reader is referred to other textbooks (e.g. Bowling, 2002; Smith, 2002; Babbie, 2007) for more detailed discussion. This section will concentrate on the application of qualitative methods and development of tools in an international context.

In an international project employing qualitative methods it is important to devise a topic guide that can be used in all participating countries. This means that the research team needs to gain considerable insight into the relevant research literature and the pertinence of issues across international boundaries and within different healthcare, pharmacy or other settings. Some of this will have been done in the early stages of project design and preliminary fieldwork, but at this stage much more depth and detail is required. Ensuring equivalence of the language employed in the topic guide will probably not have quite the same importance as in questionnaire design, as items are more likely to be listed as topics or issues, which will be explored from the perspective of respondents and therefore in local contexts, rather than specific pre-determined questions. In qualitative research the importance lies more in the relevance and comparability of meaning across the different countries. This relies on the input of research team members from all countries involved. Even though a multi-language team may conduct its written as well as verbal communication in one language, often English, not all of the relevant literature will be available in this language. The team therefore relies on each member feeding such relevant information into discussions so it is accessible to all team members. This, again, exemplifies the importance of effective communication amongst the team. To ensure that cross-country relevance and meaning is achieved, each team member needs to appraise all stages of the instrument development.

Previous researchers have identified a number of challenges when undertaking cross-cultural qualitative research (Yelland and Gifford 1995; Twinn, 1997; Kapborg and Bertero, 2002). In an evaluation study of how student nurses perceived their education in Lithuania, the quali-tative interviews were conducted by an interpreter (Kapborg and Bertero, 2002). Threats to validity ensued at various points during the interview process: it was difficult for the researcher to direct adequate probes; there was a risk that the interpreter used simplified questions that were easy to answer; there was a possibility that the interpreter could have misinterpreted some answers or coloured responses with their own interpretation. A further problem was that the responses in English may have differed from the responses in Lithuanian, since the researcher could not control whether translation was verbatim. The authors concluded that interpreters should not only have the required linguistic abilities but also be trained in the research field, and further-more, validity would be strengthened if the interpreter shared in the understanding, expectations and values of the respondent group.

Twinn (1997) reported on the complexities of translating quali-tative data from Chinese to English. First, in using different translators, different interpretations following translation of the narrative were identified, which had implications for the generation of themes and second, problems arose in the translation of words for which there was no true equivalent in the source language. Yelland and Gifford (1995) cautioned the use of focus groups as a research method in cross-cultural contexts. They found the method to be time-consuming and inhibitory amongst some participants from non-English speaking backgrounds. This they felt was influenced by the respondents' cultural expectations, e.g. that the facilitator should be treated as an expert and a reluctance to disagree with others.

Working in different countries, health systems and often languages means that potentially numerous teams and researchers will be involved in data collection and analysis. This makes it relatively difficult to 'standardise' the approach in quite the same way as when using quantitative methods, such as questionnaires. Interviews or focus groups in different countries are likely to be conducted in various languages and, importantly, by different individuals. Having a comprehensive topic guide that is relevant in all countries is only one aspect of addressing this issue. Ensuring that team members have sufficient knowledge of the theoretical as well as practical principles underpinning qualitative research is crucial and may involve some form of training. It is important that all partners employ comparable and qualitatively valid approaches through all stages of the research. Thus, it is important that sampling and recruitment are done in a similar (equivalent) way in the different countries (see Chapter 5), and that procedures of data collection and approaches to analysis are appropriately discussed, understood and agreed by all (see Chapters 6 and 7).

A further issue that needs to be raised in this context concerns the exploratory nature of the qualitative approach, where it is important to remain responsive to the issues raised during data collection. As data collection in the different countries will probably be collected concurrently, opportunity to reflect upon and respond to variation *between* countries in concepts and issues uncovered once data collection is underway will be very limited. This, again, highlights the importance of having procedures in place to ensure the consistency in approaches to, and standards of, data collection, processing and analysis.

Conclusion

This chapter has provided an overview of the principles of quantitative and qualitative research in relation to instrument development. Ensuring the validity of an instrument is a challenging task, which becomes far more complex in an international study, when it will be employed across many diverse population groups, situations and socio-cultural settings. However, the principal considerations and challenges for researchers have been discussed here. The data collected in any study can only be as good as the tools used. If the instruments are inappropriate in design or of doubtful validity, the study will be of limited value. It is worth investing sufficient time and effort in the preparatory stages of any study to the development and testing of the instruments, to ensure the international and cross-cultural validity of any conceptual, methodological and practical approaches.

References

Abbott J, Baumann U, Conway S, Etherington C, Gee L, von der Schulenburg J-M G, Webb K (2001). Cross-cultural differences in health related quality of life in adolescents with cystic fibrosis. *Disabil Rehabil* 23: 837–844.

Babbie E (2007). *The Practice of Social Research*, 11th edn. Belmont, CA: Thomson Wadsworth.

Behling O, Law K S (2000). *Translating Questionnaires and Other Research Instruments: Problems and Solutions*. London: Sage.

Bowden A, Fox-Rushby J A (2003). A systematic and critical review of the process of translation and adaptation of generic health-related quality of life measures in Africa, Asia, Eastern Europe, the Middle East. South America. *Soc Sci Med* 57: 1289–1306.

Bowling A (2002). *Research Methods in Health. Investigating Health and Health Services*, 2nd edn. Buckingham: Open University Press.

Brislin RW (1970). Back-translation for cross-cultural research. *J Cross-Cultural Psychol* 1: 185–216.

Cha E S, Kim K H, Erlen J A (2007). Translation of scales in cross-cultural research: issues and techniques. *J Adv Nurs* 58: 386–395.

ESRC (Economic & Social Research Council) (2007). *Question Bank*. http://qb.soc.surrey.ac.uk/index.htm (accessed 19 December 2007).

Francis S-A (2001). Measurements of health and illness. In: Taylor K, Harding G (eds) *Pharmacy Practice*. London and New York: Taylor & Francis, pp. 411–431.

Hupkens C L H, van den Berg J, van der Zee J (1999). National health interview surveys in Europe: an overview. *Health Policy* 47: 145–168.

Jones P S, Lee J W, Phillips L R, Zhang X E, Jaceldo K B (2001). An adaptation of Brislin's translation model for cross-cultural research. *Nurs Res* 50: 300–304.

Kapborg I, Bertero C. (2002). Using an interpreter in qualitative interviews: does it threaten validity? *Nurs Inq* 9(1): 52–56.

National Statistics (2007). *The National Statistics Socio-economic Classification*. http://www.statistics.gov.uk/methods_quality/ns_sec/default.asp (accessed 19 December 2007).

Oppenheim A N (1992). *Questionnaire Design, Interviewing and Attitude Measurement*. London and New York: Pinters Publishers.

Robson C (2002). *Real World Research: a Resource for Social Scientists and Practitioner Researchers*, 2nd edn. Oxford: Blackwell Publishers.

Smith F J (2002). *Research Methods in Pharmacy Practice*. London: Pharmaceutical Press.

Smith F J (2005). *Conducting your Pharmacy Practice Research Project*. London: Pharmaceutical Press.

Twinn S (1997). An exploratory study examining the influence of translation on the validity and reliability of qualitative data in nursing research. *J Adv Nurs* 26: 418–423.

Wang W-L, Lee H-L, Fetzer S J (2006). Challenges and strategies of instrument translation. *Western J Nurs Res* 28: 310–321.

Willgerodt M A, Kataoka-Yahiro M, Kim E, Ceria C (2005). Issues of instrument translation in research on Asian immigrant populations. *J Prof Nurs* 21: 231–239.

Yelland J, Gifford S M (1995). Problems of focus group methods in cross-cultural research: a case study of beliefs about sudden infant death syndrome. *Aust J Public Health* 19: 257–263.

Yu D S F, Lee D T F, Woo J (2004). Issues and challenges of instrument translation. *Western J Nurs Res* 26: 307–320.

5

Sampling and recruitment

This chapter discusses principles and procedures of sampling and recruitment. A sampling strategy that adheres to scientific principles of sampling theory underpins the external validity of research. In an international study the sampling strategy and recruitment procedures have to be operationalised in a number of what may be very diverse settings. For a study in just one country common sampling and recruitment procedures can usually be devised and employed. However, to achieve workable procedures in diverse locations, some local modifications to procedures may be required. What is important is that any differences in procedures do not undermine the scientific integrity of the study.

Sampling: principles and strategies

Sampling is employed to enable estimates of population characteristics to be made without recourse to information about, or from, all individuals or cases in a population. By selecting a sample, the researcher is able to conduct a more detailed study within limited resources. The findings of this study are then applied (as estimates) to the wider population from which the sample was drawn. Devising a sampling strategy that is in accordance with principles of sampling theory is essential for the external validity (generalisability) of the findings. That is, to make any claims that the findings of a study, which are based on a sample, can be applied to the wider population, fundamental principles of sampling theory must be observed. In devising procedures for an international study, whether or not the sampling procedures have to be modified in different locations, a common scientific basis (i.e. the sampling strategy) in accordance with these principles must be followed.

Methodological approaches and study design

For quantitative studies, that is, those that require the application of summary or inferential statistical procedures, a probability-based sampling strategy should be employed. In qualitative studies, which involve detailed examination of textual data relating to a small number of cases or individuals, a theoretically informed, purposive sampling procedure is more common. Study design is also an important determinant in selecting a suitable strategy.

Descriptive studies

Survey research (by questionnaire, interview, direct observation: see Chapters 4 and 6) and database analysis are examples of descriptive studies for which quantitative analytical procedures, especially summary statistics, such as frequency analyses, are commonly employed. A sampling strategy will be selected to ensure that a sample is drawn that is representative of the study population. In studies in a single country or setting, the members of a population may be easily identified and defined by a series of eligibility criteria. However, studies in a number of different countries may present difficulties in operationalising common eligibility criteria and ensuring that populations and samples are comparable.

Qualitative studies (in-depth interviews, focus groups and some studies employing direct observation or diaries – see Chapters 4 and 6) are commonly descriptive. Random sampling procedures are often not appropriate; the small sample size may lead to high sampling error. Qualitative work is also often informed by theoretical or conceptual frameworks (e.g. from the literature or policy documents) from which the researcher can make a judgement regarding the characteristics of individuals most able to provide data important to their study objectives. This will provide the basis of a sampling strategy. In studies across international boundaries however, questions may arise regarding the transferability of any theoretical or conceptual frameworks. For example, health or medicines policy, health beliefs, or other perspectives that underpin the values and practices in one place may have limited relevance in the context of other cultures and settings. In studies in several countries these differences may be pronounced, leading to difficulties in arriving at a conceptual framework, and a sampling strategy that is acceptable, relevant and therefore valid in all.

In terms of sampling, focus groups, which generally produce descriptive data on the views, perspectives and experiences of the participants on the issues under study, present additional considerations. Sampling for focus groups involves decisions regarding both the groups themselves (if relevant special interest groups already exist) and participants within them. Between six and eight participants is regarded as the optimal size, but smaller and larger groups (up to a maximum of about 12–15 participants) can also be considered (Krueger, 1994). Individuals from differing backgrounds, characteristics and experiences may be expected to hold varying views important to the study objectives and thus should be included. However, how these individuals should be represented in the focus groups will require some thought. While there may be benefit in mixing within groups, with regard to certain characteristics, in the hope of encouraging discussion of diverse issues and perspectives, there may also be a case for not mixing within the groups. For example, people from disadvantaged and affluent backgrounds may feel uncomfortable discussing affordability and cost-related issues together in the same group. Members of different health professions, e.g. doctors and nurses, or those at different points in their careers, e.g. junior and senior pharmacists, may also best be invited to focus groups with participants of similar backgrounds which are thus more likely to be conducive to open and frank discussion.

In sampling for studies employing direct observation, consideration has to be given to both the individuals within the settings as well as the settings themselves. Sampling strategies will commonly be informed by some theoretical framework. Settings will be selected on the basis of displaying particular characteristics. When observing events or activities in pharmacies, for example, researchers may aim to include pharmacies that offer varying ranges of services, differ in their clientele (e.g. serving more affluent or poorer population groups), or are of varying organisational structures (e.g. independent, part of a large corporation; or in an institutional versus community setting).

Experimental and intervention studies

The study design for an experimental study comprises intervention and control groups. In true experimental design, members of the population should be randomly assigned to either the experimental or control group and preferably be unaware of which group they are in (i.e. the study is 'blind'; if researchers measuring the outcomes are also unaware, the study is 'double blind'). This is to assure equivalence of the two groups (aside from sampling error) and to enable objective comparisons. Operationalising experimental design across a number of countries can be complicated and problematic. Decisions have to be made, such as the unit of randomisation, which must be workable in terms of sampling procedures in all locations. If these studies are to involve 'blinding' then the feasibility, ethical considerations etc. must also be separately assessed in all locations.

In health services, pharmacy and medicines use research, experimental designs involving randomisation is often not possible, and quasi-experimental designs are employed (Bowling and Ebrahim, 2005). In these studies assignment to the experimental or control group may not be random. Allocation to one or another group may be pre-determined as a result of system or practice characteristics, participant preferences or other ethical considerations. Equivalence between groups is then attempted by other methods, such as matching (finding individuals for the control group that share important characteristics with those in the experimental group), a technique that is adopted also in case–control studies. The aim of matching is to ensure that the two groups are similar in all ways that might be important in influencing the outcomes of the study (i.e. confounding factors). Of course, randomisation, if it is possible, confers greater scientific validity.

Experimental or quasi-experimental designs are commonly employed in intervention studies. A before-and-after study with a matched control group is an example of quasi-experimental design. A before-and-after study without a control group enables a description of changes following an intervention but it may not be possible to attribute these changes with certainty to the intervention itself rather than confounding factors. Diversity in healthcare organisation and provision between countries will add to the challenges of operationalising these designs.

Pilot and feasibility studies

Sampling strategies for pilot studies are often much more flexible. The goal of a pilot study is to check that data collection is workable within the proposed settings and that the data gathered will be sufficient in terms of its quality and comprehensiveness to achieve the study objectives. Researchers may feel able to make these assessments from data collected from a convenience sample. Similarly, a feasibility study may assess the operation of an intervention in a convenience or purposive sample, prior to assessment of its effectiveness in a wider range of settings.

In an international context, the selection of sites for pilot and feasibility studies may be more important. In research in different countries, a wider range of organisational, environmental, cultural and other contextual factors may impact on the feasibility and effectiveness of study procedures and workability or value of any intervention. A sampling strategy should be devised to ensure that this variability is taken into account.

Sources of data

The data required for the study will be apparent from the study objectives. Possible sources can then be considered. In health services research, data are commonly sought from individuals: health professionals and/or patients from a range of inpatient, outpatient, community-based and home settings; or the public, for which population-based sampling strategies may be required. Documents (e.g. patient notes, request forms for drug information, notifications of medication-related problems) and databases (e.g. prescribing information, patient records held in a pharmacy) are other potential sources.

Healthcare systems differ significantly between countries (Black and Gruen, 2005). The predominance of a public or private healthcare system may determine the availability of information to researchers. The coverage of a healthcare organisation may affect the extent to which information will relate to any population group. Healthcare organisational factors may affect the availability of information and/or access to datasets as well as prospective participants by researchers. For example, data on the use of medication by a population of interest may be maintained on a database in some countries, to which researchers can be granted access. In another country no such database may exist and the researcher will have to resort to alternative methods to obtain the necessary data, e.g. by surveying health professionals or patients. In Personal account 5.1, Chris Bingefors describes the need for, and development of, different sampling strategies for obtaining population-based samples to study health-related quality of life in Sweden and the UK. She also discusses attempts to assess their equivalence and consequent potential impact on the results of the study.

For many studies conducted in a single country or setting there may be a number of options regarding the possible ways of obtaining data. Each would have its own strengths and weaknesses. However, a single source of the relevant information, sampling strategy and procedure would ultimately be identified, the task of the researcher being to select the best approach.

Sampling and recruitment procedures will be influenced by the availability of information sources which will be a reflection of healthcare systems and other features of the provision, delivery and uptake of

PERSONAL ACCOUNT 5.1
KERSTIN (CHRIS) BINGEFORS

Comparing countries in population studies – is it possible?

The aim of this study was to compare health-related quality of life (HRQoL) in population subgroups between countries. The present project concerns Sweden and England and Wales (Bingefors *et al.*, 2005).

HRQoL was measured using Eq5D and SF-36 in postal surveys to samples of the population in Sweden and in England and Wales. The samples may suffer from differences in representativeness. The Swedish sample was drawn statistically from the very exact population register covering all individuals resident in the country, and is considered very representative of the total population. It is also possible to do an extensive analysis of non-responders (response rate 66%) and include weights in the analysis to compensate for non-response. Socio-economic factors important for the study such as married/single, income and educational level are taken from central registers and not from respondents' answers. Unlike the Nordic countries, England and Wales lack comprehensive and reliable population registers, therefore, the sample was taken from households on the electoral register. The individuals in the sample were then asked whether they wanted to participate in a panel. The response rate in the final panel relative to the original population is not possible to calculate with a comparable method. Information on important factors was collected from respondents. The question is whether there are substantial differences in attrition and in data quality between the two samples.

Can we then conclude that differences in HRQoL between the countries found in the study are real differences or are they due to differences in the samples? One method of quality control is to include question items in the survey that can be checked against other data sources in the country. If results from the survey, for example mean age, gender distribution, mean income and educational level, match population information from other sources, we can make a reasonable judgement as to the representativeness of the sample and of the HRQoL results found.

Reference

Bingefors K, Isacson D, Koltowska-Häggström M, Kind P (2005). Grumpy old men or happy young women. *Qual Life Res* 14: 2019.

care, access to medicines, and organisation and operation of pharmacy services in the different locations of the study. A sampling strategy considered optimal in one setting may be inoperable in another. What is important is that sampling procedures are in accordance with agreed sampling strategies and, as far as possible, comparable datasets are achieved. If sources of information in different settings are of limited comparability, this will jeopardise the validity of comparisons between groups, the combining of datasets and hence the scientific integrity of the research.

Populations and sampling frames

The study population refers to all the individuals to whom the study relates. For example, a study among users of a particular medicine, would aim to involve a representative sample of all users of the medicine, so that the study findings would be applicable to all. In this case the population would be all users, and the job of the researcher would be to devise a sampling strategy that would achieve a representative sample (preferably random in quantitative studies). It will be important to agree a definition of the study population, including detail of inclusion and exclusion criteria, prior to developing the sampling strategy. This will enable members of the research team to assess the reliability and validity with which eligible participants will be identified by any sampling procedure.

Sampling is most straightforward if a suitable sampling frame can be found. A sampling frame is a list of all the members of a population. If such a list is available it can be used as a basis for the selection of the sample. In studies in different countries, the availability of comparable sampling frames cannot be assumed. Examples of sources of sampling frames to obtain a population-based sample in the UK are the postcode address file, electoral registers and lists of patients registered with general medical practices. However, such registers, although commonly held in many countries, may be incomplete or not up-to-date, especially if registration is not mandatory. When a suitable sampling frame is not available, alternative sampling strategies will have to be devised. In developing countries, greater problems can arise as reliable systems may not be in place. For example, to investigate healthcare practices at a household level in Ghana, because of the absence of a suitable sampling frame, the first phase of a study entailed researchers visiting selected villages identified from town offices and mapping and then numbering all houses so that a sampling frame could be constructed and a random sample could be drawn.

Many countries may have registers of pharmacists, but differences may exist in the make-up of these lists. Some lists may include only active practitioners, or professionals with certain qualifications, or those who work in particular sectors of the profession. Some lists may include (but not distinguish) individuals no longer resident or practising in the country concerned, who may be viewed as ineligible, which would result in a poor apparent response rate. The profession/workforce may be structured in different ways (for example: pharmacists, prescriptionists, technicians) which will have implications for the comparability of sampling frames. If membership of professional bodies is voluntary rather than mandatory, the lists will be self-selecting rather than comprehensive, which will affect the extent to which they are representative of the population of interest. Sampling frames may also vary in how complete and/or up-to-date they are. Therefore, for each country or research site a separate appraisal of the available sampling frames will be required: who it includes (compared with those of other countries), and an assessment of its comprehensiveness and reliability.

Special interest groups, clinic lists or pharmacy patient records in different settings may include differing spectrums of individuals. All potential sampling frames will have their merits and compromises. The task of the researcher is to be prepared to spend time at the start of any study to identify possible ways of accessing the population groups of interest and carefully appraising the comparability and validity of the different options in their own country, before comparing these across the different countries. In her personal account, Frances Owusu-Daaku describes the experience of sampling for a study among Ghanaian women living in Ghana and the UK (Personal account 5.2).

PERSONAL ACCOUNT 5.2

FRANCES OWUSU-DAAKU

Health-seeking behaviour: perspectives of Ghanaian women in London and Kumasi

---

Ghana, a West African country and former British colony, has a population of about 20 million people. Healthcare in Ghana is characterised by pluralism: allopathic, herbal and spiritual approaches may operate concomitantly. Britain has a National Health Service funded from general taxation and is free at the point of use for virtually the whole population. At the time of the study allopathic care was provided in a 'fee for service' system in Ghana. A National Health Insurance Scheme has now been introduced but has not received full national coverage after its official launch in 2004.

The study aimed to describe and compare the perspectives of health, health-seeking behaviour and use of medicines by Ghanaian women resident in London, UK, and Kumasi, Ghana (Owusu-Daaku and Smith, 2005). This was to identify ways in which Ghanaian women adjusted to a different system and/or retained their own perspectives regarding healthcare and use of medicines.

Some challenges

- *Sampling frames:* In neither country was there a suitable sampling frame. Documentation in Ghana is scanty. Documentation of Ghanaian residents in the UK could not be relied upon because there is no register of Ghanaian immigrants. Since this was a qualitative study, a snowball approach to sampling was adopted, to identify individuals who had been in the UK for different periods of time, were of different ages, family structures, with and without a long-term illness, etc.
- *Language barriers:* This had a potential impact on the representativeness of the sample (in Ghana) and the interpretation of the data. About 66 languages are spoken in Ghana, in addition to English, the official language. The language largely spoken in Kumasi is Twi, and therefore only those who saw themselves as fluent in either Twi or English were interviewed. This could have excluded some potential respondents. Also, where interviews were conducted in Twi, translations had to be extensively reviewed to ensure that the meaning of texts and not just words were accurate.
- *Conducting the interviews:* One interviewer conducted all the interviews in both countries, which simplified problems of consistency in approach. However, the interviewer had to be alert to meanings 'between the lines' for the UK residents with respect to racial discrimination and to seek for clarification. In Ghana, some respondents were reluctant to talk about the attitude of healthcare workers, unless they were prompted to do so. The interviewer, a pharmacist, had to be tactful about sensitive issues so that she was seen in a 'neutral light', especially in relationship to healthcare workers.

A surprise!

Almost every respondent in London was eager to participate, despite a busy schedule for most of them. The interview was seen as an opportunity to talk with a sympathetic ear about issues that would not have been expressed otherwise. Thus, the response rate was good.

Reference

Owusu-Daaku F T K, Smith F J (2005). Health-seeking behaviour: perspectives of Ghanaian women in London and Kumasi. *Int J Pharm Pract* 13: 71–76.

Sampling procedures

Sampling procedures can be distinguished as those that are probability-based and those that have other scientific or a less scientific foundation.

Probability samples

A probability sample (based on the principle of random selection) is one in which every member of the population has a known probability of being selected into the sample. A random sample is the ideal. In a simple random sample, all members of the population have an equal chance of being selected.

Simple random sampling

Simple random sampling is the most straightforward procedure, but it requires a sampling frame. It generally involves numbering all members of the population (in the sampling frame) and the generation of random numbers to select the individuals that will form the sample. The required sample size, sometimes expressed as a sampling fraction must be agreed.

A systematic selection procedure is sometimes employed. This involves the selection of, for example, every 2nd, 4th or 10th individual (depending on the sampling fraction required). This is sometimes used in settings when an advance sampling frame is not available, although the eligible population is clearly identifiable; e.g. selection from successive attendees at a clinic, clients in a pharmacy, etc. This procedure can aid the data collection process, for example, enabling spacing of interviews throughout a data collection period. However, it is important to ensure that there is no systematic ordering in which individuals/cases present, which would lead to systematic bias in the sample. An independent assessment of the practicability and validity of the procedure would need to be made for each site.

Common variants of simple random sampling are stratification (of the population) prior to selection of the sample, and cluster sampling. These procedures are adopted to improve representation of different sectors of a population (stratification) or to improve the feasibility of the research process. In both cases, randomisation remains a feature.

Stratified random sampling

Stratification involves dividing the population into sub-groups prior to sample selection. It can be useful in small samples in which sampling error could result in inadequate representation of some sub-groups, or where differential response rates between some sub-groups might be expected. The population is generally stratified according to those variables believed to be important to the study objectives. The researcher then knows that there will be sufficient numbers in each group to enable comparisons to be made. To select cases/individuals from each strata a simple random sampling procedure may be applied to each, so that a stratified random sample results.

The strengths of stratification are reflected in the frequency with which the procedure is adopted. However, in studies conducted in different countries and systems some further considerations arise. First, are the same population sub-divisions relevant in all settings? If healthcare or pharmacy services are structured differently, what is an important classification in one country may not apply in another. Age may be an important determinant of medication-related behaviours in one country, but in others (e.g. where age-related eligibility for exemption from payment for prescription medicines does not feature) other factors such as socio-economic variables may be a more important basis for stratification. A second consideration is whether or not the necessary information for stratification is available in all countries. For example, data on key variables may not be maintained in all locations, or it may not be accessible to researchers. Where information is available, are the measures used comparable? Third, does the stratification result in similar-sized population sub-groups in all locations? Some statistical analyses will require minimum numbers in each sub-group.

Cluster sampling

A cluster sample is one in which the data collection is concentrated in a number of discrete locations. Thus, in any international study, the locations involved already comprise a series of clusters. The basis for the selection of these countries/locations should be clear to an outsider. This may have been the result of a meeting of minds of individuals (self-selection and opportunistic), or the sites might have been selected on the basis of some theoretical considerations. In many cases the research process (which must be both workable and address real questions) will mean that aspects of both approaches feature.

In a cluster sample the participants are drawn from, or 'clustered' within, a number of sites. Ideally, in cluster sampling, the sites should be randomly selected from the total population of eligible sites. Thus, a cluster sampling process is also commonly multi-stage. Stage one is the selection of the locations for the study, a second stage may involve the selection of sites within each of these locations, prior to a final stage which will be the selection of participants or cases.

The benefits of cluster sampling are in the management and execution of the research. Participants are confined to a small number of locations (and possibly sites within them) rather than being dispersed over a large geographical area. This often allows a more efficient and effective data collection. It may also enable the involvement of a larger sample overall. A larger sample size, to some extent, may off-set the loss of generalisability that results from restricting sample selection to a limited number of locations. Unless data can be gathered effectively remotely (electronically or by mail) cluster sampling is often necessary to gather sufficient data.

Measures to ensure that cluster sampling is representative of the population are important. Thus, random (probability) sampling procedures should be followed at all stages if possible. If a small number of locations are to be selected, it may be important that these reflect diversity within the population as a whole. Thus, stratification and cluster sampling procedures are sometimes combined.

In studies across international boundaries, separate sampling strategies and procedures may be required in the different sites. This may apply to the numbers of clusters, characterisation of the clusters, and strategies and procedures for the selection of participants. In all cases instructions must be clear so that they can be correctly followed. Careful notes should also be maintained in all settings as to how procedures are operationalised in each location.

Non-probability sampling procedures

A number of non-probability sampling procedures may be employed. In studies in which the scientific validity and generalisability may not be paramount (e.g. pilot or feasibility studies) greater flexibility in procedures may be acceptable. However, in general, procedures should be agreed and carefully documented. This will ensure that they are appropriate to study objectives and how they are operationalised can be taken into account when interpreting the results. Quota samples (from which some level of representativeness may be argued) and convenience samples are examples of non-probability samples.

Theoretically informed and purposive samples

These are commonly employed in qualitative studies. Selection of the sample is guided by some theoretical or conceptual framework which indicates the characteristics of participants that are most likely to be in a position to provide the information that is required to meet the study objectives. In a study across diverse locations, separate sampling strategies and procedures may be required. Confirming that any theoretical or conceptual framework is relevant across different international settings is important to the ultimate validity of its application. Any modification of sampling strategy or procedures should be balanced against its impact on the comparability of data between sites and integrity of the study.

Sample size

Sample size will be governed by the aims and objectives of the study. Sampling error is a consequence of sample size, smaller samples being open to greater potential sampling error and less precision in the study findings.

A sample size calculation will be needed for a randomised trial in which a pre-determined probability of detecting a difference between groups is desired. Similarly, a descriptive study in which the research team wish to achieve a level of precision when drawing inferences from a sample and applying them to the wider study population will require a minimum sample size. Sample size determination involves a power calculation based on estimates of variation between groups or cases on key variables and the level of precision required in the results. Guidance on sample size calculations may require the assistance of a professional statistician; further information can be found in many statistics texts (e.g. Florey, 1993; Kirkwood and Sterne, 2003).

In multi-centre studies, especially in diverse locations or when common study procedures cannot be applied, determination of required sample size is complex. Study objectives must be clear. There will be within-group and between-group variation to be taken into account, possible differences in population structures and variability in sample characteristics. Studies which will require the application of specific statistical procedures may benefit from professional statistical advice.

In exploratory studies, a less robust approach may be appropriate. The research team may want to ensure that all sites are 'fairly' represented by either proportionate sampling (a common sampling fraction in all sites) or recruitment of a given number of cases in each. If comparisons between study sites or other population sub-groups are proposed, then it is important that sufficient data are collected from each.

The research team may wish to ensure that datasets from each location are separately adequate in that they can stand alone in providing useful information for each location, in addition to being combined to provide an overall picture. These goals should be reflected in the study objectives, which will provide a framework for decisions regarding the sample size.

Saturation sampling is a further approach sometimes employed in qualitative studies. In this technique, sampling and recruitment continues until no new themes or issues emerge in the data. This is an appropriate approach in exploratory studies where the aim of the research is to identify perspectives and concerns in relation to a topic from the viewpoint of respondents. Once the researchers believe that all relevant themes and perspectives have been uncovered, then no further data are required. In an international study saturation sampling could mean that sample sizes vary between locations. As data collection and analysis will to some extent be concurrent, researchers in the different countries will need to liaise during the course of the study to ensure that data collection and analytical procedures in all locations adhere to common conceptual frameworks.

Sampling bias

Sample characteristics in relation to the study population are determined by the sampling strategy and procedures. To some extent, the sampling procedure itself may preclude the participation of certain individuals. For example, sampling in pharmacies may lead to poorer representation of people who are house-bound or do not usually use pharmacies; and decisions would need to be made as to how to handle proxy visits (people who come to the pharmacy for medicines or advice on behalf of someone else). Surveys in clinics may include a higher proportion of regular attenders. Household surveys may include a lower proportion of people in employment outside the home. The extent and nature of potential sampling bias can sometimes be deduced and it may be quantifiable.

In studies in different countries a number of additional concerns may arise which could jeopardise the validity of the research if not adequately addressed. First, the extent of bias between sites may differ, which may mean a separate appraisal of potential bias is required for each site. Second, the nature or profile of bias may vary. Even if agreed sampling procedures are carefully applied in all settings, there may be subtle differences in the characteristics of the populations. Structural, environmental and other contextual factors could lead to differences between populations, which will result in non-equivalence of samples.

Sampling bias is a systematic predisposition to the exclusion of certain population groups as a consequence of the sampling strategy. Unlike sampling error, which is a result of random error in sampling procedures, it cannot be reduced by increasing the sample size.

Recruitment of participants

Uniformity between locations

Once the sampling procedures have been detailed, the next task is the recruitment of participants. The study population will be defined by the inclusion and exclusion criteria. These criteria determine the characteristics of the population and have to be operationalised as recruitment procedures in all locations. For this, it must be possible to interpret and apply the eligibility (inclusion and exclusion) criteria in all sites. If they cannot be applied in each setting this may threaten the comparability of the samples from each location. For example, if a criterion for inclusion is the level of severity of disease, or use of particular medicines, this information will be required at the recruitment stage to identify eligible prospective participants.

The development of common recruitment procedures in all sites in an international study may not be possible or desirable. Systems of healthcare provision may determine the most appropriate recruitment procedures. The availability of sampling frames, access to information, and the organisation of professional practice and operation of healthcare vary greatly between countries. An effective approach in one setting may be impossible in another. Indeed, Mary Tully's personal account illustrates the impact that the structure and organisation of pharmacy services in different countries can have on sampling and recruitment as well as other aspects of a study such as access to, and reliability of, data (Personal account 5.3).

In an international study different procedures may be required to identify eligible participants. In some places a sampling frame may be available which provides sufficient information to enable the research team to identify prospective participants. In other locations a different approach may be required, for example, a screening tool may be

PERSONAL ACCOUNT 5.3

MARY TULLY

Choosing community pharmacies

I was working with two Swedish colleagues to conduct research, using simulated patients, into the quality of counselling on prescribed medicines in community pharmacies (Beckman-Gyllenstrand *et al.*, 2007). Clearly, we wanted a sample that was as representative as possible of all pharmacies in Sweden – a large country with huge variation in population density between north and south. I expected it to be relatively easy to choose a random sample of pharmacies that were stratified by location (rural, suburban or central) and geography, and indeed it was. From my UK perspective, however, I was not expecting easily to find much, if any, information on busyness (such as turnover of prescriptions and over-the-counter medicines). I did not count on the influence that Apoteket AB might have on research possibilities.

Apoteket AB is the company that, at that time, owned every pharmacy (community and hospital) in Sweden. They also employed the vast majority of pharmacists; my two Swedish colleagues either worked full or part time within the quality or research divisions of head office. When we were identifying variables for the study, I expressed my negativity about being able to get commercially sensitive information such as turnover of community pharmacies. However, this was not a problem. Apoteket AB collected this information centrally and was very willing to allow us to use it in the study – after all they had commissioned the work. In addition, when I suggested that it might be hard to find out who had spoken to the simulated patient and whether they were a pharmacist or not, again I was looked at in amazement: 'But they will have signed the label that they spoke to the patient – why wouldn't you be able to find out? And if you can't read it, they will have a name badge.' We were not only able to find out who was working in the pharmacy that day, but also whether they were a pharmacist or another grade of staff, their qualifications and their age (no guesstimating based on appearances). So we had much greater confidence in our data for the regression analysis as to the factors influencing provision of counselling than I might otherwise have expected.

Reference

Beckman-Gyllenstrand A, Tully M P, Bernsten C B (2007). Factors influencing the provision of poor counselling for prescribed medicines in Swedish community pharmacies. *Int J Pharm Pract* 15 (suppl 1): A27–A28.

employed to confirm eligibility prior to recruitment to the research. In some situations, a 'proxy' measure may be available; for example, use of a particular medication may be used as an indicator of a diagnosis.

Ethical requirements, in different countries, in particular requirements to maintain confidentiality of patient information, will influence access to sampling frames which include personal information (see Chapter 3). Whether or not the research team can be granted permission may determine the level of involvement they can have in selecting a sample and conducting the recruitment. Researchers may have to liaise with practitioners (who have legitimate access to patient records) in the recruitment, and only when prospective participants have agreed to take part will any information be available to the research team. Involving practitioners presents them with an extra burden; it also limits the ability of the research team to monitor the extent of adherence to protocols (in recruitment procedures and maintaining records on recruitment and non-response). In terms of response rates, a recruitment procedure that relies on prospective participants being pro-active in expressing their wish to take part generally results in lower response rates.

The recruitment procedures need to be agreed, checked for feasibility, validated and documented for each location. It is important to ensure that variation in procedures between countries does not threaten the comparability of data and the scientific integrity of the study as a whole.

Communication with prospective participants and documentation

The documentation for prospective participants may include letters of invitation and information sheets detailing the purpose of the research, what it will involve, who is conducting the work, assurances of confidentiality, etc. Depending on the nature of the study and ethical requirements, reply slips (and sometimes consent forms) may also be included for participants to indicate if they wish to take part. These documents, while including much common content, will usually have to be tailored to each location (see also Chapters 3, 4 and 6 for further discussion).

In addition to documentation for prospective participants, it is good practice to inform stakeholders and interested parties in all countries. A range of 'courtesy letters' may be prepared for this. The endorsement and/or co-operation of interested organisations and individuals may be beneficial to the execution of the study, including response rates. Because of differing professional structures, healthcare organisation and range of interest groups, each location may devise its own list of contacts. In some cases, organisational structures will determine access to the population and sample. For example, to contact practising pharmacists it may be necessary to go through an employing organisation.

Response rates

Securing an adequate response rate can be the greatest threat to the success of a study (Smith, 2002). All aspects of the recruitment procedures should be devised with a view to maximising the response rate. One hundred per cent response rates are rarely obtained and any level of non-response leads to the possibility of response bias. It is to be expected that in an international study, response rates will differ between locations. A response rate that is satisfactory overall may mask very low response rates in one of more of the study sites. This will affect the external validity of the study overall as well as accentuating the impact of differing profiles of non-response between sites.

Response bias arises because responders and non-responders (individuals who are and are not agreeable to participating in a study) differ in some way. It is acknowledged that in general, individuals who agree to take part in a survey are more likely to have an interest in the subject matter, or perceive the study as relevant to their concerns. Because a higher proportion of these individuals respond, the respondents will be atypical of the wider population in these important respects, which results in response bias. To assure the external validity of the findings of a study, some assessment of response bias is necessary. This can then be taken into account when interpreting the findings and generalising the study to the wider population. A number of approaches can be taken to maximise response rates and minimise response bias.

Maximising response rates

Recruitment and data collection procedures that will encourage rather than discourage participation should be devised. Thought should go into the format, timing and content of information to prospective participants, the aims of the research, the potential benefits to others if not themselves should be clear. In some studies face-to-face contact to explain the purposes and procedures of a study may encourage participation. Data collection procedures should be devised to minimise the burden on participants. Questionnaires should be as brief and relevant as possible and easy to complete. Interviews should be no longer than necessary, arranged at a time and location convenient for interviewees. These issues are discussed further in Chapters 4 and 6 in relation to instrument development and data collection.

It is usual practice to send out reminders (often two) to non-responders (see Chapter 6). If possible the research team should maintain a record of responders and non-responders, so that repeat mailings can be targeted. The achievement of acceptable response rates should be addressed in the preliminary fieldwork and pilot stages. Participants in these stages can be asked to comment on recruitment procedures and data collection methods, identifying aspects that they might find attractive or off-putting. Investigation of low response rates at a pilot stage may provide the research team with an opportunity to consider the reasons for this and how procedures might be modified. In an international study securing as high response rates as possible should be addressed at both international and individual country level. There may be cultural or healthcare organisational factors particular to specific countries that may be anticipated to influence response rates.

Maintaining data on non-response

Maintaining records of numbers of non-responders and when possible documenting reasons for non-response enables rates to be determined and may provide some indication of the likely generalisability of findings and how responders and non-responders may differ (Smith, 2002).

In a study in a number of locations these data should be collected in all. The level of non-response may differ between sites, which will have implications for both combining data from the different sites and interpretation of findings locally. However, it is not only the number of non-responders that is important, but also their make-up. In the context of international research, variation in the profile of non-response across sites should also be assessed.

Proformas for the collection of data on non-responders are important in all studies. Where a uniform set of sampling and recruitment procedures are employed, a proforma should be normal practice. Although in studies across multiple sites and settings, data available on non-responders will vary, some assessment of response bias, including differential response bias across different sites, will greatly enhance the value of most studies.

Follow-up of non-responders and comparison with respondents

Active follow-up of non-responders (beyond the usual reminders) to assess key characteristics enables an assessment of the nature of response bias. Confidentiality of personal information precludes this in many studies, but when it is possible it is valuable. In international studies where recruitment procedures vary, follow-up of non-responders may be possible in some sites but not others. However, any information on the possible nature of response bias may be helpful in assessing possible bias in the study findings. In some instances an indication of response bias may be possible by comparison of responders with the wider population. In questionnaire studies, researchers have compared the responses of early and late responders, on the assumption that differences between these groups are likely to reflect differences between responders and non-responders.

In most studies in health, pharmacy and medicines use, response bias is an important potential problem. While efforts to achieve high response rates, documenting response rates, assessing levels and profiles of response bias are important to all studies, in a multi-centre study, especially where datasets and research procedures are not entirely uniform, the problems and implications become more complex.

In an international study, research protocols should detail how these issues are to be addressed in each site. The time and resources required attending to issues of non-response and response bias should not be under-estimated. A careful documentation of response rates and assessment of consequent potential bias will greatly enhance the validity and value of many studies.

Conclusion

Appropriate sampling and recruitment strategies underpin the external validity of the research. Ideally, common procedures should be employed in all locations. In an international study, the diversity of patterns of healthcare provision, professional structures, availability of sampling frames, ethical requirements and other considerations may mean that this is not possible. However, it is important that a common overall sampling strategy is identified that observes fundamental principles of sampling theory. Furthermore, response bias ought to be minimised and every effort made to ensure good response rates in all countries, as this will affect the validity of any data collected and the possibility for cross-country comparison and interpretation.

References

Black N, Gruen R (2005). *Understanding Health Services*. Maidenhead: Open University Press.

Bowling A, Ebrahim S (2005). *Handbook of Health Research Methods*. Maidenhead: Open University Press.

Florey C du V (1993). Sample size for beginners. *BMJ* 306: 1181–1184.

Kirkwood B, Sterne J (2003). *Essential Medical Statistics*. Oxford: Blackwell Science.

Krueger R A (1994). *Focus Groups: a Practical Guide for Applied Research*. London: Sage.

Smith F J (2002). *Research Methods in Pharmacy Practice*. London: Pharmaceutical Press.

6

Data collection

This chapter will discuss the different ways of collecting data in health services, pharmacy and medicines use research projects. It is of paramount importance in international studies to maintain common procedures across all sites, so that scientific integrity is maintained both within each location as well as in terms of a combined dataset. A wide range of data collection methods may be employed in research into healthcare, medicines use and professional practice. This chapter will focus on the most common, highlighting their strengths and weaknesses and particular challenges of their application in international studies.

Covering letters, information sheets and consent forms

Any data collection method that involves identifiable individuals requires that they are adequately informed. This applies whether they are involved as 'active' research participants, such as those being observed, interviewed or surveyed, or 'passive' subjects, where their personal (medical) data may be used in a way that cannot guarantee anonymity. As discussed in detail in Chapter 3, voluntary participation and expressions of informed consent are fundamental requirements of ethical research practice. Information that allows people to make an informed decision about whether they want to be involved in a study or not will need to include relevant details about the research and be in a form that can be understood by prospective participants.

The information about a study that tends to be provided includes: a covering letter inviting individuals to participate in a study, an information sheet/leaflet, and consent form. As highlighted in Chapter 3, some tailoring of information for individual study sites may be necessary, either because of local contexts in which the data collection is being conducted and/or the requirements of different ethics committees. As these documents are not part of the data collection tools, they do not need to be exactly the same in all countries. However, the information that should be provided will be similar across all locations (also see Chapter 5).

Potential participants should be informed of the purpose of the study, why and how they have been selected, and what is asked of them if they take part. They should also be assured that any personal information and all study data will be kept confidential, i.e. not shared with anyone outside the research team, including (if applicable) health professionals who are involved in their care. It should be clear that participation is voluntary throughout, and that they may withdraw at any time, without their healthcare being affected. They should know who is responsible for the study and who they can contact for further information (also see Chapter 3).

Participants need to be assured that any personal information will be stored and handled in accordance with the individual countries' data protection regulations. For member states of the European Union this is based on legislation passed in Directive 95/46/EC (European Commission, 2007), which in the UK has been implemented in the Data Protection Act of 1998. In the USA data protection is governed by the Privacy Act of 1974, 2004 edition (United States Department of Justice, 2007); and similar laws and regulations exist in other countries. The UK's National Research Ethics Service (NRES) has produced guidance on information sheets and consent forms, and outlines the information that should be conveyed to any potential participants. This includes the purpose of the study; how the individual was selected; what the study will involve, including potential risks and benefits; that participation is voluntary and withdrawal possible at any time; assurances of confidentiality and ethical review; who is funding and responsible for the research; how the results will be used (NRES, 2007).

In an international study, it may also be appropriate to inform patients that the research is part of an international project, and how the results from the different countries will be used. If data are to be transferred between countries, participants ought to be informed about this, along with confirmation that no information from which an individual can be identified will be included. The need for combining datasets from different locations should be clear from the objectives of the study.

The careful preparation of information for prospective participants and subsequently, its effective communication, is essential to the fundamentals of informed consent, i.e. participants' informed agreement to participate in the study (see Chapter 3). Obtaining this in a formal manner is not always necessary; for example, the completion and return of a questionnaire is commonly taken as implying consent. However, for more involved studies, such as participating in interviews, focus groups and observations, it is good research practice (and in many countries, including the UK, it is a requirement of ethics committees) that formal informed consent be sought. This procedure requires the preparation of a consent form. The participant (and often also the investigator) will sign a copy of the form, one to be kept by the investigator and one by the participant. An example of a UK standard consent form can be found in the NRES's guidance on information sheets and consent (NRES, 2007). Requirements, guidelines and cultures may differ in different countries and ought to be explored at an early stage (see Chapter 3).

Maintaining records regarding the recruitment of participants, response rates and non-responders

Irrespective of the data collection method employed, information should be collected at all study sites on the recruitment of participants, response rates and as far as possible any characteristics of non-responders and/or reasons people choose not to participate. To ensure consistent information is maintained, some common recording procedures and forms should be developed. This information may enable some assessment of response bias: the likely impact of non-response on the representativeness of the sample (see Chapter 5).

The higher the response rate, the lower the probability of systematic bias resulting from differences between the responders and non-responders. In an international study, the response rates between sites may differ, and hence the representativeness of the participants in each. Maintaining records on recruitment and response will enable some assessment of this for each site as well as for the combined dataset.

Similarly, if obtainable, data on the characteristics of non-responders, or reasons why people choose not to take part, may provide some indication of the nature of bias (i.e. profile of non-responders). In an international study, this too may differ between locations. If relevant information is collected in all study sites, some site-specific assessment will be possible. This, again, will help ensure valid interpretation of the data and conclusions of the study.

For other aspects of the data collection, documentation relating to the operation of the research should be maintained. Such information will help identify instances in which protocols were not, or could not be, followed as well as indicating where and how study execution was more or less successful. As will be apparent from the following discussions relating to the operation of different data collection methods, maintaining these data may also be a valuable part of the quality assurance procedures regarding the conduct and operation of research across international settings.

Survey research: questionnaire administration

In Chapter 4, the principles of survey design and development were discussed including translation if necessary, validation (in terms of face and construct validity as well as translational equivalence and cross-country relevance) and piloting. Once the instrument has been developed it is then employed as a tool of data collection. In an international study this means administration of the questionnaire to equivalent samples in the different countries, which will have been identified using agreed sampling frames and procedures (see Chapter 5).

As outlined in Chapter 4, there are three main methods of administering a survey questionnaire: self-administered questionnaires (where respondents complete the questionnaire themselves), questionnaires administered in the form of face-to-face interviews, and those conducted by means of a telephone interview. Each method has its own advantages and disadvantages.

Self-administered questionnaires

The most common procedure for administering a self-completion questionnaire is by post, where a questionnaire is mailed, accompanied by a covering letter and/or information sheet and a self-addressed envelope for return to the investigator. In international research it should be remembered that the reliability and coverage of postal services can be very variable. Effective distribution in some less-developed countries may require the hire of private taxi or courier services. With accessibility to computers and the internet, questionnaires can sometimes effectively be distributed by e-mail, either inviting return by e-mail or, more commonly, on-line completion. An advantage of the latter is that respondents' entries are logged electronically and can be fed directly into the database that will be used for storage and/or analysis, such as SPSS (Statistical Package for the Social Sciences).

Questionnaires for self-completion are sometimes distributed by hand. For example: to clients in a pharmacy, at a local GP surgery, or a hospital clinic or ward. This may be in accordance with a pre-determined probability sampling strategy (see Chapter 5), or to a 'captive' or convenience sample, e.g. pharmacy students following a lecture or at a meeting of a special interest group. These latter approaches commonly confer more limited generalisability.

Questionnaire response rates and follow-up mailings

Regardless of the way in which self-administered questionnaires are distributed, it is rare that all people in a sample will complete and return questionnaires. As a rule of thumb, one can expect that around one-third to one-half of the sample will return the questionnaire following an initial mailing. There are a variety of reasons for not returning questionnaires, and an important one is that completion and return is too much trouble, being low in terms of a respondent's priorities. Therefore, anything that makes it easier to return questionnaires should improve response rates. Providing pre-paid (or Freepost) addressed return envelopes is common practice, while offering the option of completion on-line will be attractive to some respondents. Attention should also be paid to the questionnaire itself. If it is of poor design, too lengthy or complicated, lacks face validity (i.e. appears to the respondent to be irrelevant or ask the wrong questions) this may be reflected in the response rates. Refer to Chapter 4 where the importance of designing a succinct, relevant and interesting questionnaire was discussed.

There are ways to increase response rates, and probably the most common one is to send out reminder mailings, which should include a further copy of the questionnaire. Reminder mailings are usually sent around three weeks apart. Because of the importance of maximising response rates, identification numbers should (whenever possible) be included on questionnaires so that completed forms can be matched with individual respondents. Excluding such identifiers from a questionnaire in the hope of improving response rates does not generally pay off. Being unable to assess response bias is usually a serious limitation to any study. This can be a further disadvantage of distribution among captive populations. In an international study the local researchers will usually manage the distribution and repeat mailings of questionnaires. Timings and procedures may be modified according to the characteristics of each setting. Incentives are also sometimes used to boost response rates, the ethical issues and potential impact on the study of these were raised in Chapters 3 and 5.

Assuming that a reliable and valid instrument has been devised, poor response rates will usually be the greatest threat to the success of survey research. Forethought, time and effort should be invested in achieving the best rates possible. The value of careful preparation of appropriate and attractive materials and sensitive approaches to potential participants cannot be overemphasised. Studies with low response rates may not produce any meaningful results; they may also be difficult to publish. But what is a good or acceptable response rate? The answer to this will probably depend on a variety of factors, such as the sampling strategy, ability to make some assessment of potential response bias, whether the study, although flawed by low response, adds to existing knowledge in the subject area. Response rates can be extremely varied, even between seemingly similar populations, as exemplified in a review of pharmacy practice studies (Smith, 2002). Maximising response rates during recruitment, problems of response bias and assessing its impact when analysing data are discussed further in Chapters 5 and 7.

Collecting survey data by interview

Collecting survey information by means of an interview can be done either face-to-face or by telephone. The main difference from self-completion questionnaires lies in the fact that an interviewer takes the respondent through the questionnaire in a structured manner and records responses on their behalf. This means that the interviewer can clarify questions to ensure relevant responses. For some studies, especially when survey instruments are semi-structured, data collection in a face-to-face interview results in much more meaningful data and would be the preferred method.

To ensure that a similar approach is adopted between interviewers and in all interviews, detailed directions for the conduct of interviews and/or training should be provided. The highly structured nature of questionnaire surveys needs to be maintained, and each interviewer needs to be a 'neutral medium', with all interviewers posing the questions in the same way, thus avoiding interviewer bias. In international studies this will merit special consideration as diversity in settings may provide greater opportunity for variation in interpretation of questions leading to non-comparability of data. It is, therefore, important that all interviewers share a common view regarding how questions should be asked and what clarification should be provided in relation to incomplete or unclear responses. Additionally, within each location, consideration should be given to issues such as the environment of the interview, the demeanour or affiliation of the interviewer and other factors that might affect the success of the data collection in a specific location or setting.

Face-to-face interviews tend to achieve higher response rates than self-completion questionnaires. However, they are generally more costly and time-consuming. Time and resources are required not merely to administer the questionnaire, but also to arrange the interviews, and travel to and from the venues. Thus, when interviewers are involved in data collection for a questionnaire survey, sample sizes are likely to be smaller and prospective participants less widespread geographically (cf. cluster sampling in Chapter 5).

Telephone interviews

One advantage of telephone interviews is that they are considerably cheaper and quicker to conduct, as no travel is involved. While they can be an effective method for brief and very structured instruments they can have a number of limitations. They are, of course, restricted to people who have telephones. If the sample is pre-selected and telephone numbers can effectively be obtained for the identified individuals, then sampling bias should not occur (although there will still be response bias). However, many numbers may not be listed in publicly available directories; in any household, pharmacy or other workplace certain individuals may more commonly take calls. Some people opt only to have a cell-phone (mobile). In an international study, coverage, access to telephones and ownership of cell-phones can be very variable between countries. Although probably cheaper than face-to-face interviews, there may be some resource implications for making calls to cell-phones.

In terms of conducting a telephone interview, other issues arise. Knowing you have the respondent's attention and obtaining considered responses can be a problem. Obtaining focused responses to specific questions can be difficult, especially as the respondent cannot see the interview schedule, and has no concept of its length, or the direction and nature of subsequent questions. Some of these problems can be overcome by advance arrangements regarding a suitable time for the telephone interview, being explicit about the time completion is likely to take, and/or sending a copy of the questionnaire prior to conducting the interview.

In an international project it may be that different approaches are required between locations depending on the characteristics of each, and the expected success of particular methods. What is viable in one location may not be in another. It is also possible to use telephone interviews to boost the response to a questionnaire otherwise mailed for self-completion. If different methods are employed, this is not necessarily a problem and may be the only way of achieving satisfactory response rates or successful data collection. However, careful thought must be given to the likely impact of different approaches and methods on the reliability, validity and comparability of data.

Qualitative research: interviews and focus groups

Study design and sampling strategies commonly employed in qualitative research have been discussed in Chapter 5. Here, the focus is on the application of principles of qualitative enquiry to data collection, in particular in setting up and conducting qualitative interviews and focus group discussions, which are the most commonly employed methods. Special considerations to ensure a scientific approach is maintained in the data collection in international studies will also be highlighted.

The development of a topic guide that is relevant to the settings and contexts of all partner countries and that can be successfully employed in all was discussed in Chapter 4. The importance of adequate training and expertise in undertaking qualitative research was also emphasised. While well-established in pharmacy practice and related research in some countries, qualitative approaches and techniques are very unfamiliar in others, a situation described by Ellen Schafheutle and Karen Hassell in Personal account 6.1.

In quantitative research, once a valid instrument has been developed, the scope for interpretation and exercising judgement is limited. Survey research relies on structured instruments, the scientific reliability and validity depends on the quality of the instruments. It is not intended that these should be employed flexibly.

In contrast, data collection in qualitative interviews and focus groups is a highly skilled task. As described in Chapter 4, interview schedules or topic guides for qualitative interviews, which may be described as semi-structured or unstructured depending on the extent to which the direction of the interview is pre-ordained, generally impose a very limited structure on the data collection and are sometimes relatively brief. Commonly, they comprise principally open questions to introduce a topic for discussion; subsequent questions depend on the issues raised by interviewees in response to these open questions and therefore cannot

PERSONAL ACCOUNT 6.1
ELLEN SCHAFHEUTLE AND KAREN HASSELL

Co-ordinating focus groups in seven European countries

In 1998–2001 we were involved in an EU-funded project within the ENDEP (Evaluation of National Drug European Policies) group, in which Professor Peter Noyce was the UK partner. Six (originally seven) countries participated: Austria, Finland, France, Germany, Italy, the UK (and the Netherlands). The aim of the project was to explore whether the cost to patients for their medicines (in the form of co-payments/prescription charges or over-the-counter prices) had an impact on how patients managed their condition, and if, and how, this medication cost affected the way physicians prescribed for these patients. The study focus was on patients who had hay fever, dyspepsia or hypertension, or used hormone replacement therapy (HRT), thus including symptomatic and asymptomatic conditions, as well as ones where self-medication options were available.

At the time, sufficient evidence existed (particularly from North America) to suggest that medication costs reduced patients' medication use, but little was known about the why and how, and whether physicians had a role to play in this. The project involved both patients and physicians, and included a qualitative stage employing focus group methodology (which preceded a quantitative one: a patient survey – see Personal account 4.2 on page 61 – and a physician conjoint analysis) and for which the UK team provided the so-called 'reinforced action' because they had the relevant experience and expertise. This meant that, despite the French partner being the overall 'project lead', and all partners providing so-called 'concerted action', the methodological training and design for this aspect was co-ordinated from the UK.

The research was conducted in five different languages and the ENDEP countries all had different healthcare systems, with varying degrees and combinations of public and private healthcare provision and, specifically, different types of prescription charges/co-payments (as well as availability of over-the-counter medication). These all had to be accommodated in the design and execution of the project.

This account is specifically about the first part of the ENDEP project, the qualitative focus groups in seven countries (Weiss *et al.*, 2001; Schafheutle *et al.*, 2002; Hassell *et al.*, 2003). The country partners came from very different professional and research backgrounds (e.g. economists, health economists and health services/systems researchers). Many were used to handling large (often secondary) datasets, some had experience with primary data collection using surveys, but only the UK team was experienced in the use of qualitative methods. The UK team, therefore,

continued overleaf

Personal account 6.1 (continued)

provided 'reinforced action', which was delivered in the form of an initial intensive two-day workshop in Manchester, UK, accompanied and followed by supportive documents and proactive as well as responsive verbal and written advice.

As there was so little expertise in qualitative methods among the other project partners, relatively strong and continued support was required from the UK team. Through discussions amongst the partners regarding the study focus and relevant issues, we drew up a focus group topic guide, which was amended and agreed. We also provided guidance on sampling and recruitment, appropriate to the objectives and qualitative approach of the research, for example how to identify and select eligible physicians and patients in each setting, while ensuring that the groups in the different countries would include similar groups of people (e.g. in terms of prescription cost issues and likely affordability of medicines). Much discussion and support took place on how to conduct a focus group discussion: especially the role of the facilitator as enabling discussion rather than guiding or leading it.

To address the insecurities amongst the partners, who worried about their lack of experience in the conduct, analysis and reporting of focus group discussions, the UK team conducted a 'pilot' focus group with physicians and used the transcript to develop a framework for analysis (listing themes and categories), analysed the data and wrote a report. All of these documents were distributed to all partners as a guide to focus group methodology. The 'pilot report' was particularly useful in providing a template for analysis and report-writing for all partners, demonstrating the structure, the level of detail that was required and the use of quotes to support findings. The 'pilot' report also proved helpful to partners in promoting cross-country quality and comparability of final reports. This was important because partners had to depend on these rather than the original transcripts, which were only available in the individual country's language.

References

Schafheutle E I, Hassell K, Noyce P R, Weiss M C (2002). Access to medicines: cost as an influence on the views and behaviour of patients. *Health Soc Care Community* 10: 187–195.

Weiss M C, Hassell K, Schafheutle E I, Noyce P R (2001). Strategies used by general practitioners to minimise the impact of the prescription charge. *Eur J Gen Pract* 7: 23–26.

Hassell K, Atella V, Schafheutle E I, Weiss M C, Noyce P R (2003). Cost to the patient or cost to the healthcare system? Which one matters the most for GP prescribing decisions? A UK-Italy comparison. *Eur J Public Health* 13: 18–23.

be pre-determined. Thus, rather than undertaking an administrative task (cf. mailing of a questionnaire survey, or conducting an interview that does not deviate from a pre-determined question structure) the qualitative interviewer operates almost as a 'research instrument' themselves. In accordance with the spirit and principles of qualitative enquiry they have to gather all the relevant information, sometimes with limited guidance from within the instruments. A central feature of qualitative enquiry is that data collection aims to provide an opportunity for interviewees to present their perspectives in the context of their priorities, concerns, experiences, desires, etc. The interviewer should leave their own views and thoughts behind, providing an opportunity for the gathering of data from the viewpoints of the respondents.

Thus, it will be apparent that data collection in qualitative studies requires a high level of expertise. In an international study, the experience of researchers in different locations in qualitative research may be very variable. This may be a reflection of the research culture in different settings and the extent to which qualitative work is understood and valued. So, unlike survey research, where a methodologically sound instrument renders achieving acceptable response rates as the principal challenge, in qualitative research the scientific validity depends on the application of skill and expertise in the data collection process. Assuring the universal observance of principles of qualitative enquiry across diverse settings will be an important concern in the data collection of an international study.

In their personal account, Janine Traulsen and Anna Almarsdóttir describe how they uncovered and addressed problems of cross-cultural differences in international focus group research (Personal account 6.2). Because of the different languages of participants, translation was required. Their experiences describe how in validating the translation process, 'translation of data' as a technical task, could be distinguished from the 'meaning of the data' which was an interpretive one. The approach and processes they adopted to translation, along with a technique of 'interviewing the moderator (facilitator)' led to the identification of different organisational, social and cultural contexts between settings that were important to the interpretation and analysis of the data.

Setting up qualitative interviews and focus group discussions

Face-to-face individual interviews in qualitative research differ from those of a structured interview in that they are often longer, require more

PERSONAL ACCOUNT 6.2

JANINE TRAULSEN AND ANNA BIRNA ALMARSDÓTTIR

Culture and language in focus group research: interviewing the facilitator

We began working together as a team in the mid-1990s. Our first collaborative project was a multi-method evaluation of the change in legislation in the pharmacy sector in Iceland. The methods used were focus groups, in-depth interviews, surveys and secondary analysis of statistical data.

Our method of interviewing the facilitator grew out of at least two problems facing us when employing focus groups. The first was the need to pilot and make the necessary adjustments to the first focus group we had conducted as quickly as possible. The second problem was the need for the research team, which was multidisciplinary, multinational and multilingual, to optimise the face-to-face time they had together (we were living and working in two different countries). In the first project, the research team consisted of three pharmacists and one sociologist, all four spoke Danish and English and only three spoke Icelandic.

Interviewing the facilitator started out quite spontaneously, immediately following the very first focus group, as a form of debriefing of the facilitator by the other members of the research team (Traulsen *et al.*, 2004). We found that interviewing the facilitator had special advantages in a multinational and multilingual study. First, it minimised the language problem – i.e. the focus groups were carried out in Icelandic and the analysis and dissemination were completed in English. From the beginning we agreed that the dissemination of the results would be in English, and therefore it was important for us to have the data translated as quickly as possible.

Second, it forced the natives (in this case the Icelandic researchers) to reflect on, and explain, cultural differences. As the famous anthropologist Edward Hall pointed out, we can only come to grips with our own culture when being confronted by a new and different culture (Hall, 1977). In this case when the non-native interviewed the native focus group facilitator the discussions were not mere 'translations' of what was said but rather an exercise in describing to an outsider what was 'normal' and what was 'abnormal' in the focus group discussions. For example, when the participants were asked about having their health records used in research they never mentioned problems of confidentiality. This surprised the non-Icelandic team member who asked the facilitator why this was so. It turned out that with a population of only 300 000, most Icelanders felt related to each other and they did not feel that they had any secrets at all, either from each other or from the state – a fact of life which did not seem to bother them at all (Almarsdóttir *et al.*, 2004). This cultural dimension would never have emerged had it only been Icelanders doing the study –

they would never have questioned responses, which, to them, appeared normal.

References

Almarsdóttir A B, Traulsen J M, Björnsdóttir I (2004). 'We don't have that many secrets' – the lay perspective on privacy and genetic data. In: Árnason G, Nordal S, Árnason V (eds) *Blood and Data – ethical, legal and social aspects of human genetic databases.* University of Iceland.

Hall E T (1977). *Beyond Culture.* Garden City, NY: Anchor Books.

Traulsen J M, Almarsdóttir A B, Björnsdóttir I (2004). Interviewing the moderator: an ancillary method to focus groups. *Qual Health Res* 14: 714–725.

considered responses from the interviewee and greater attentiveness by the interviewer. Interruptions are more likely to be disruptive and result in lost data. In a noisy or distracting environment concentration may be difficult to maintain. Audio-recording is common in qualitative interviews and the venue must allow effective audible recording. It is usual to arrange interviews (time and location) to suit the convenience of the interviewee. As long as a suitable space is available this may be the respondent's home, place of work, a private room or a quiet location in a hospital, health centre or pharmacy. In an international study, suitable places and arrangements for interviews will need to be separately identified in each case: for example, when interviewing pharmacists the availability of a private room or quiet area may be usual in some countries, while not in others. Similarly, some pharmacists will be sole operators and unable to leave the pharmacy for any period, while for others this may not be a problem. For each location, satisfactory arrangements should be identified which will enable interviews to be conducted according to agreed criteria. In the project report, the place, environments and settings of interviews in each study site should be described.

Focus groups have to be arranged in venues and at times that are suitable for a number of people. They need to be convenient to get to, comfortable and allow a private discussion in a quiet environment without interruption. Suitable venues may be conference venues, community facilities, hotels or public houses; participants can also be invited to come to a university department hosting the research. Some groups are also convened in health centres or hospitals, which may be particularly useful for staff. However, there is some concern that conducting focus groups with 'patients' in a clinical environment may hinder a free and frank discussion of health and medicines-related issues.

Conducting qualitative interviews and focus group discussions

In both interviews and focus groups it is important that the interviewer or focus group facilitator maintains control, which means that they manage the process, i.e. keep the discussion focused on issues pertinent to the study objectives. While achieving this, the interviewer or facilitator has to keep an open mind. What may appear irrelevant material regarding the study objectives to the interviewer, may turn out be of great importance from the perspective of the interviewee. When conducting the interview or focus group, the interviewer must remain attentive to the issues raised by the respondent(s), be ready to request further detail, background information, clarification of events or circumstances, personal feelings, outcomes, etc. They should be ready to follow-up any passing comments made by an interviewee that may allude to an experience or viewpoint of possible relevance. Interviewers should be comfortable with 'silence' in the interviews, i.e. to provide an opportunity for an interviewee to gather their thoughts or attempt to recall relevant information. In their questioning it is important that interviewers are non-leading. It is helpful if the instrument includes a series of neutral questions that can be employed to gather further information on any topic. For example, 'Please tell me more about . . .'; 'How did you feel about that?'; 'How did that situation arise?'

In the case of focus groups, the facilitator also needs to ensure that more verbose participants do not dominate the group, and equally, that quieter participants are offered the opportunity to contribute. Thus, in a focus group discussion, further questioning may include: 'Has anyone else had a similar experience?'; or 'Does anyone have a different view on this?' Equally, as group interaction and discussion is an important feature and strength of focus groups, the facilitator needs to know when not to speak, so that the discussion can flow without unnecessary interruption.

If interviews or focus groups are conducted by researchers with limited experience of qualitative research, examples of neutral probing questions within an interview guide can be immensely helpful. Considerable expertise and proficiency is required to formulate non-leading probing questions, without any prior preparation or thought, to examine issues, experiences and events from the perspective of respondents, and achieve the level of detail required. The interviewer or facilitator needs to be careful not to display views of their own which may influence responses of others. Experienced researchers advocate that the interviewer (or facilitator) needs to be actively reflexive about their own role in the interview or focus group process to ensure that any bias from him/her is minimised. Needless to say it is crucial that the interviewer or facilitator is familiar with the topic guide, so that they are prepared for discussions not necessarily to proceed in a pre-set order. This also allows the discussion to be flexible and responsive regarding any theme, particularly if the topics are raised by participants without prompting.

Interviews and focus groups will usually be audio-recorded and later transcribed verbatim. While the primary purpose of audio-recording is to enable qualitative analysis, in the data collection stage it allows the interviewer to concentrate on the actual interviewing, picking up cues and ensuring comprehensive data are gathered on all issues rather than having to concentrate on taking detailed notes. In focus groups it is not uncommon to have a co-facilitator present. The co-facilitator can take different levels of involvement, from overseeing the smooth running of the event, such as organising catering, or distributing expenses forms (for travel and incentive payments) and/or brief background questionnaires, to co-facilitating the discussion. It can be useful if the co-facilitator takes notes during the focus group, to aid the interpretation of the transcribed data, identify contributions made by the same participants and note non-verbal responses or contextual factors. It can also be valuable for the two facilitators to debrief immediately after the event, sharing their perspectives on the content and operation of the discussion. If audio-recording is continued during this time, this may be helpful in informing the analysis.

Observation

Observation studies in health services research are those in which the researcher is present at the study site, and observes and records information relevant to the study objectives. An observer can thus record events or behaviours as they occur in their natural environment. This avoids some of the disadvantages of other methodologies, such as questionnaire surveys and interviews, which rely on participants' subjective self-reports, or where memory may be a problem which potentially introduces so-called recall bias. In questionnaires or interviews, respondents may also be tempted to recount behaviours and events in such a way that they appear in the best possible light. Direct observation is particularly useful when observing routine behaviours, where respondents are not necessarily aware of their behaviours, or act without much conscious thinking. Asking about such 'hidden' behaviours in interviews or questionnaires does not always yield the most useful insights.

Qualitative and quantitative observations

Observation studies may be quantitative and/or qualitative in approach. Quantitative observation studies will have a clear focus on exactly what events or behaviours are to be observed, and a structured instrument, generally in the form of a recording sheet, will have been designed. The development of this will follow many of the principles that apply to questionnaire design. For example, categories for recording events or behaviours of interest need to be relevant, exhaustive and mutually exclusive (see Chapter 4). In international studies, instruments must be equally relevant, applicable and operational in all locations. Quantitative observations will then produce comparable data on relevant events. For example, details of events as they occur will provide information on their frequency. Recording what is being done at certain predetermined time points also enables an analysis of what tasks individuals (e.g. pharmacists) are performing and how often (cf. work sampling studies).

Qualitative observation studies involve an examination of events or behaviours within their natural environment, i.e. in the context of constraints and facilitating factors. Thus, qualitative approaches in international studies enable the diverse characteristics and their impact in the different locations to be examined in context. Data will often be collected in the form of detailed field notes, which will not only record events or conversations etc. that take place, but also non-verbal behaviours, descriptions of the environment, situations or circumstances in which they occur, such as the presence of other people or other potentially influencing factors. Audio- and video-recording is sometimes used. Field notes will also provide insights into the observer's feelings and views on why he or she thinks certain events or behaviours are occurring, and these notes should be clearly differentiated from those recording observations. They can be very useful pointers for the analysis of data and provide an example of qualitative analysis that commences during data collection. This early analysis can inform the subsequent data collection in terms of the observations and associated contextual information that should be recorded (i.e. an iterative process of data collection and analysis, see Chapter 7). Field notes need to be detailed. In some situations, a surreptitious approach to data collection has to be devised.

As with interviews, the high level of skill required for such a reflexive approach will be apparent. It will present particular challenges for international studies, especially in ensuring that a full research team has an opportunity to influence decisions that will have implications for the uniformity of data collection procedures, ensuring similar standards in the execution of the study and ultimate comparability of datasets.

Observation studies can be either participant or non-participant. Non-participant means that the researcher observes and records activities and behaviours as an outsider. The majority of observation studies in pharmacy practice have been non-participant, and many (but not all) have been quantitative (Smith, 2002). Participant observation has its origin in anthropology, where a participant observer lives, works and participates as a member of the community being researched for the duration of the data collection period, often for extended lengths of time. These types of observation study therefore tend to be qualitative.

Reliability and validity in observation studies

Whether a quantitative or qualitative study employing a participant or non-participant observer, data collection involving direct observation of events presents potential concerns in both reliability and validity. In terms of reliability the observer has to interpret and operationalise the data collection instruments. According to the protocol and objectives of the study the observer has to decide what events and behaviours to observe, and in relation to these situations, what aspects to record and how. In quantitative studies this should present few problems. Provided the data collection instruments are well designed and clear regarding the types of events and details to be recorded, consistent information should be obtained. Some comparisons of data collected by two different observers can provide a measure of inter-rater reliability and highlight where problems may arise, such that the instrument or specific directions regarding its use can be clarified. In international studies it is likely that many different researchers may be involved in an observation study.

Checking for uniformity in the application of research instruments in international studies is possibly both more challenging and more important. There may be logistical problems in providing the same training sessions for observers at all sites. Opportunities for observers from all locations to share their experiences of employing an instrument so that a common approach can be identified may be limited. Diversity between settings in which the instrument and observation procedures are used is likely to be pronounced, reflecting differences in healthcare systems and delivery of care, professional roles and socio-economic and cultural perspectives of local communities. Thus, steps must be taken to ensure the relevance and consistent application of data collection instruments and procedures across sites.

In qualitative observations the researcher needs to ensure that a systematic approach to identifying, observing and recording events is being taken; e.g. by following up unexpected observations or those that seemingly contradict earlier interpretations. The researcher will be guided by both the study objectives and data collection instruments. Again, in an international study there will be considerable scope for varying interpretations of what constitutes a relevant event. In some cases this will be valid in terms of the study objectives, as the nature of events will be determined by the contexts in which they occur. In a qualitative study, the aim may be to identify how and why different events arise in different settings, rather than to attempt to incorporate events in all locations within a common framework.

The Hawthorne effect

Researchers in both qualitative and quantitative observations need to reflect on their role, and how their presence and actions may influence the behaviour of those they are observing. This phenomenon is termed the 'Hawthorne effect' and although it can probably not be entirely eliminated, efforts can be made to keep it to a minimum. The Hawthorne effect can be due to the mere presence of a researcher, knowledge that a study is taking place or, indeed, awareness of the study focus. Consequent changes in behaviour will be both intentional and inadvertent. There is some evidence that in many situations, even if participants' behaviour is influenced at first, it does eventually revert to usual, once they have become accustomed to the researcher's presence. Particularly in qualitative studies, researchers may aim to be present for extended periods of time, although how long this should be is difficult to predict and will depend on many factors which will vary between studies, across settings, and individuals.

To minimise the Hawthorne effect, a non-participant observer should be as discreet as possible, keeping any interference in usual routines and interaction with subjects to a minimum. Some researchers also decide not to inform the research subjects of the exact study purpose, as knowledge of this may make them reflect on the behaviours under investigation and thus change their behaviour. However, depending on the topic under investigation, it may be deemed unethical not to inform study participants fully and thus not allow them to give informed consent to participation, or the option not to participate. In the research and professional literature there has been debate on the ethics of covert investigations. The acceptability and feasibility of the different approaches may also vary between countries and settings within them.

Finally, it is worth mentioning that simply observing actions and behaviours is not necessarily enough to understand why these behaviours are occurring. Observing the events in the contexts of the environments and circumstances in which they occur may provide some clues but rarely full explanations. Observation studies are therefore often not employed as a sole method of investigation, but combined with interviews in the hope of identifying further insights into specific events and behaviours. The timing of any such interviews would be important, preferably following the periods of observation as otherwise it could sensitise the respondent, leading to greater behavioural change. However, if too delayed, events will no longer be fresh in the minds of respondents.

Bryony Dean Franklin in her study (Personal account 6.3) employed structured non-participant observation methods to compare medication administration errors in hospitals in the USA and UK. She describes a number of conceptual and practical issues that arose. These included the difficulties of achieving a common definition of a medication administration error, variation in the names, formulations and availability of products, different working practices and ethical issues as a consequence to necessary differences in study methodology.

It will be apparent from the discussion here that observation studies across international sites will present many challenges. Preserving reliability by aiming for standardised procedures could threaten the scientific validity conferred by incorporating and documenting wider contextual factors pertinent to different locations. There will also be operational issues, the feasibility of employing similar or differing procedures in each location. However, if potential difficulties in arriving at a common conceptual framework and methodology can be overcome, observation is a powerful tool.

PERSONAL ACCOUNT 6.3

BRYONY DEAN FRANKLIN

An observational study of medication administration errors in a UK and a US hospital

Our experience relates to an observational study of medication administration errors (MAEs) in a US and a UK hospital (Dean *et al.*, 1995). The two countries use very different systems for prescribing, dispensing and administration of medication for hospital inpatients. We therefore wanted to conduct a comparative study of the incidence and types of MAEs, using the same methods, definitions and researchers. The methods involved observing nurses preparing and administering medication, and comparing the medication administered with that prescribed. We were fortunate in being able to link up with Barker and Allan, experts in the field from the USA (Allan and Barker, 1990). US researcher Allan and UK researcher Dean each carried out some data collection in each country and liaised closely to ensure that methods were consistent and applicable across both settings. Aside from setting up the study, the main challenges related to MAE definition, differences in drug names and formulations, different working practices, and an important ethical issue. Each of these will be discussed in turn.

First, we had to adopt an MAE definition that could be applied in both settings. We found that there were many different working practices which meant that issues that would be considered an error in one country would not be in the other. For example, leaving medication in a tablet cup at a patient's bedside for subsequent self-administration would have been considered an error by US nursing staff. However, although considered poor practice in the UK hospital, it would not have been considered an error at the time of the study. We therefore did not include this as an error in either country. We had to develop detailed lists of what would, and would not, be considered an MAE in our study, to ensure that the same criteria were used throughout.

Second, there are many differences between the two countries in terms of drug names, formulations and the availability of products. Observation of medication administration requires rapid identification of the medication being administered, and these differences did create practical problems for the two researchers who each had to gain familiarity with the products available in the other country.

Third, the different working practices meant we had to use slightly different data collection methods in each country. In the UK hospital, medication was administered from a drug trolley which was wheeled from bed to bed. There was only one drug trolley on each ward at the time of the study, and the observer could remain with the drug trolley and observe medication being administered to every patient in turn. In contrast, in the USA, nurses each administered medication to their own patients, collecting individual doses from a drug trolley which remained in the treatment room. Several nurses could therefore administer medication at any one time, and the observer could only observe a proportion of all doses given. We therefore developed a strategy for sampling nurses in the US hospital, and longer periods of observation were required to gain a comparable sample size.

Finally, and most significantly, comparison of the medication given with the original medication order could only be done retrospectively in the US hospital, and concurrently in the UK hospital. In the US, the original medication orders were written in the patients' medication notes, and were not available at the time of medication administration. However, in the UK, nurses used the original medication orders, in the form of the drug chart, to determine the doses due. This difference had important ethical implications, as the pharmacist observers were likely to be aware of errors as they occurred in the UK hospital, and therefore in a position to intervene, but not in the US hospital. We decided to intervene in either country whenever the observer felt that they were in a position to prevent an error from harming the patient. We did not intervene for very minor errors. This meant that although we intervened more often in the UK hospital, relatively few interventions were made even in the UK, resulting in less potential bias.

The study was fascinating to conduct, and gave us many useful insights into the challenges of conducting international research, as well as answering our original research question.

References

Allan E L, Barker K N (1990). Fundamentals of medication error research. *Am J Hosp Pharm* 47: 555–571.
Dean B S, Allan E L, Barber N D, Barker KN (1995). Comparison of medication errors in a UK and a US hospital. *Am J Health-System Pharm* 52: 2543–2549.

Diaries

Diaries are another method of collecting prospective data. Maintained over a period of time, they constitute a chronological record or log of specific events or activities, such as illness episodes, health actions or incidents in a practice setting. They are particularly useful for gathering temporal information where the real time relationships between events and activities may be important to the study objectives; for example, to assess patterns of uptake of health services, or the relationship between illness episodes and use of both formal and informal healthcare (Hassell *et al.*, 1998). Thus, a series of events can be documented and subsequently examined for relationships. Diaries are also valuable for capturing data on events that are difficult to access by other methods. For example, rare events may require lengthy periods of observation to obtain sufficient data. In an interview focusing on retrospective events and activities, the reliability of information relating to the temporal relationship of events and actions may be questionable. Diaries can provide first-hand and insider accounts of situations that would be impossible or impractical to obtain in other ways.

Diaries may be employed in quantitative or qualitative studies. In quantitative research, the directions to participants must be very precise. If an aim is to report the frequency of events as well as other characteristics, participants may be requested to make daily entries into a diary to ensure this information is captured. All participants must have a clear view of the types of situations, events and activities to be recorded, as well as the specific information and level of detail that is required. Consistent use of the diaries between individuals and study locations will be of paramount importance. In designing the diary that forms the research instrument, many of the principles and rules of developing unambiguous and valid instruments that apply to other structured methods (e.g. questionnaires, quantitative observation, see Chapter 4) should be followed.

When used to gather qualitative data, the diary may be much less structured. However, it will be equally important that all participants understand the aims and objectives of the study, recognise the situations, events and activities that are of relevance, identify them when they occur, and provide the required information with the specified level of detail.

Ideally, recording should occur during or soon after the event, and this should minimise recall bias as a consequence of poor recollection or retrospective reflection. Diaries rely heavily on respondent co-operation, as they require a relatively high level of involvement, sometimes over an extended period of time. Attrition can be a problem and data quality can be affected by failure to maintain the diary, with consequent missing data. It is thus not uncommon to use some form of incentive, often in the form of financial remuneration, to encourage completion. However, this can have the unwanted effect of promoting retrospective documentation. In addition, a phenomenon termed 'conditioning' can occur, where study participation may either influence perceptions of relevant events, associated actions and/or the way in which they are reported. This can lead either to sensitisation, where participants display increased reporting due to heightened awareness, or fatigue, which can be conscious or subconscious and can lead to decreased reporting with time.

Diaries require very clear, explicit instructions as well as continuous encouragement. These may be delivered in a combination of letters, information sheets, but also telephone calls or e-mails which serve to explain, encourage and remind. In the context of an international study, the use of diaries as a data collection tool can be time-consuming and costly in terms of instrument development and testing, follow-up of participants during data collection, and quality assurance to ensure adherence to study procedures and comparable datasets. Furthermore, data processing and analysis can be complex.

Documentary research

The preceding sections have focused on a number of qualitative and quantitative methods involving the collection of primary data, that is, data that are obtained directly from study participants for the purposes of the research. This section will consider a different approach to data collection: that of using documents or datasets already in existence, as this may well be a basis for an international research study. Most commonly, such documents will be written or printed records, however they can also be audio and visual image records, including those available on the internet. Such documents are rarely produced for research purposes, but they can be viewed or analysed as sources for, or of, research (Bowling, 2002). Thus, in this respect, they correspond to two different approaches to documentary research.

Official records, such as those collected by governments on demographic and disease/health characteristics of the population provide some population-based data. Other documents include records relating to individual patients, e.g. patients' medical notes or prescribing or dispensing records, which provide a source of information on aspects, or users, of health services or medicines. Even though it is often accepted that these records may be incomplete, the information contained in them is usually taken as trustworthy.

Using documents or the information contained within them is probably the most common application of documents for research in national and international pharmacy and health services research projects. When relying on these secondary data sources, rather than collecting primary data to meet the study objectives, a number of questions arise. In international studies, these difficulties are likely to present greater problems than a study in a single country. The researcher has to make an evaluation of whether all important information is available to address the study objectives. The datasets from each country are likely to differ in terms of the information (variables) included. The level of precision in records and/or the extent of missing data must be assessed. The quality of the data may be unclear, in addition to varying between locations. When possible, some investigation of these difficulties is desirable and can be undertaken during data processing and analysis (see Chapter 7).

Documents can also be used as sources *of* (as opposed to *for*) research. Investigators holding a phenomenological perspective emphasise that social 'facts' are characterised by their meaningfulness to individuals in their social worlds (a particular qualitative approach). Thus 'reality' can be viewed as socially constructed through the interaction of individuals, and it is the processes and product of this which merits the research attention (Bowling, 2002). This approach, although not a common component of international research collaborations, may be very valuable. Documents of a country (for example policy documents in the area of the study focus) may provide 'an insider view' pertinent to a country or setting that may be very constructive in informing the study focus, objectives and methodology. In personal account 2.1 (page 10) Tina Brock and colleagues describe their attempts to gain information in different countries regarding the involvement of pharmacists in smoking cessation programmes. Cross-country comparison of policies and debates governing professional practice and/or health services provision, for example, may provide significant and unexpected insights into the place and operation of professional activities within different organisational, social and cultural contexts.

Combining methods in a research study: triangulation

Triangulation refers to the application of different approaches or methods within a single research study. In particular in international studies, early exploratory work may be particularly important to identify differences between settings which may affect the value of the study and or the feasibility of methods in particular locations. In addition to ensuring that research questions are relevant and applicable in all participating countries, this and other chapters have emphasised the importance of ensuring that samples are drawn in such a way that they are similar, that data collection tools are equivalent, so that data are ultimately comparable. Nevertheless, it will be apparent that in an international study it may not be possible or advisable to force a universal approach and common procedures across all sites. Some compromises and tailoring to local settings will be required if the study is to be successful. Thus, in some instances a variety of methods may necessarily be employed within a single research study. However, in devising the data collection methods, as for all other aspects of the study, the researcher must not lose sight of the study objectives and the need to achieve comparable datasets. When it comes to the analysis, careful thought should be given to the validity of combining datasets that may have been collected using varying approaches and methods.

While to achieve feasible data collection procedures across all sites, some variation in methodology will be required, different approaches and methods may also be employed for specific purposes within the course of a project. For example, exploratory approaches are commonly employed in the early stages of a research project to gather data which will inform the development of a structured instrument. Conversely, semi-structured interviews may be employed to examine the contexts of unexpected findings in a questionnaire. To achieve a series of complementary research objectives, a range of approaches may also be required. For example, observation may be employed to document activities in a pharmacy, while interviews may enable those involved to provide explanations for their actions.

Triangulation is also employed as a means of validation; and this is true to its real meaning. The principle is that by measuring phenomena in different ways and comparing the data, more accurate estimates will result. When applied to research, data relating to events, actions or behaviours may be collected in different ways. For example, observation in a small number of sites may be employed to validate self-reports in a questionnaire; a series of interviews may be conducted to check the completeness, reliability or validity of data maintained in clinical notes or other documents.

Conclusion

A wide range of data collection methods may be employed in research into health services, medicines use and professional practice. All have their advantages and disadvantages and particular concerns that arise in the context of international studies. The most common approaches to data collection have been included in this chapter together with the most important considerations regarding their validity and reliability. For any research study the generic approaches that have been discussed here will need to be applied or adapted to meet particular study objectives and ensure their feasibility in the context of any study setting. In an international study it will be apparent that operationalising common protocols across diverse settings will present additional and pronounced challenges.

In an international study, the goal of a research team will be to balance consistency in approaches and methods against their feasibility and acceptability in all study locations. In this respect, some compromises may be inevitable. The important task of the research team will be to ensure that an effective and workable set of procedures is devised and agreed such that: study objectives are met, the study is executed to consistently high standards and according to agreed protocols, the required level of comparability in datasets is maintained and that the implications of any compromises in the consistency or scientific integrity can be justified and assessed.

References

Bowling A (2002). *Research Methods in Health. Investigating Health and Health Services*, 2nd edn. Buckingham: Open University Press.

European Commission (2007). *Justice and Home Affairs – area of freedom, security and justice*. http://ec.europa.eu/justice_home/fsj/privacy/overview/index_en.htm (accessed 19 December 2007).

Hassell K, Rogers A, Noyce P, Nicolaas G (1998). *The Public's Use of Community Pharmacies as a Primary Health Care Resource*. The School of Pharmacy & Pharmaceutical Sciences and The National Primary Care Research & Development Centre. University of Manchester. Report for the Community Pharmacy Research Consortium. Royal Pharmaceutical Society of Great Britain, London.

NRES (National Patient Safety Agency and National Research Ethics Service) (2007). Facilitating and promoting ethical research. http://www.nres.npsa.nhs.uk/ (accessed 19 December 2007).

Smith F J (2002). *Research Methods in Pharmacy Practice*. London: Pharmaceutical Press.

United States Department of Justice (2007). Privacy Act of 1974, 2004 ed. http://www.usdoj.gov/oip/04_7_1.html (accessed 19 December 2007).

7

Data processing and analysis

Data processing and analysis follow the collection of data. Data processing refers to those activities that prepare the data for analysis. This includes organisation of the data, development of coding frames, coding the data and, in many studies, entry of data into a software package to aid the analysis. Each stage of the data processing requires some quality assurance procedures, including checks on the reliability, and the validity.

In international studies, additional considerations arise from the intention to combine 'independent' datasets from different locations. The combining of data may occur at various different stages during data processing. For example, the raw data (e.g. the actual returned questionnaires) may be collated in one location prior to the commencement of the data processing and then all coding and analysis is undertaken as for a single dataset. Alternatively, data may be collated, coded and entered into a database 'in situ', and the different national datasets combined to enable analysis of a combined international database. In some studies, all data processing and analysis may be undertaken within each study location and just the findings of the study compared.

The combining of datasets will require arrangements concerning the logistics of creating a combined database from the datasets in each location. Each study location may wish to retain 'ownership' over its own data and the ability to conduct its own 'local' analyses. However, to fulfil the objectives of an international study, acceptable and feasible arrangements for merging the datasets must be agreed.

International studies will also present additional complexities in the data processing and analysis. Different quality assurance issues may arise in different settings which will require their own investigations and assessment in the datasets. Modifications to study procedures and instruments to accommodate local circumstances may present additional questions regarding the validity of combined analyses and interpretation of results.

This chapter presents an overview of the common data processing and analysis procedures that are employed in health services and medicines-related research studies, and the steps that may be taken to ensure the reliability and validity of data and procedures. Its particular focus will, of course, be on special considerations in international studies.

Survey research

As discussed in Chapters 4 and 6, survey research is probably the most common approach in research into health services and medicines use for which quantitative methods will be applied. The instruments (questionnaires) will generally comprise principally closed rather than open questions. The first task of the data processing will be to devise a coding frame and to code the responses prior to entry into a database, following which some statistical procedures will usually be applied (Field, 2005).

Development and application of a coding frame

A coding frame for a questionnaire consists of a list of 'variables', which generally corresponds to the questions in the questionnaire; and associated 'values' (codes), which relate to all possible responses. The variables in a questionnaire may be 'nominal', i.e. the values applied are just labels (e.g. 1 = male; 2 = female), 'ordinal', where numeric order indicates progressively higher real values (e.g. 1 = daily; 2 = weekly; 3 = monthly, etc.) or 'interval' (e.g. numbers of prescription-related problems, respondents' ages, blood pressure, etc.).

A series of codes may also be assigned to variables relating to aspects of the research process. In general, each returned questionnaire (referred to as a case) will be given a code which acts as a unique identifier. Codes may also be included to indicate when the completed questionnaire was received (e.g. whether after initial mailing, first or second reminder).

A variable will usually be included in which nominal codes are applied to identify data relating to each location of the study (e.g. 1 = Finland, 2 = UK, 3 = Ghana). This would enable some comparative analyses of data from the different locations. Additional variables and codes may refer to place of data collection within each country. In an international study, there may be additional considerations pertinent to one or more centres which should be recognised in the coding frame. For example, in some locations it may be appropriate to include a variable to denote the mother tongue of the respondent. There may be questions for which the series of possible responses necessarily has to vary between countries. For example, there may be a different range of ethnic backgrounds or cultural identities which the study instruments and hence the coding frame should reflect. Or, it may be important to distinguish between different healthcare organisation structures relevant to different countries, which may be important to the interpretation of the data.

In general, developing a coding frame for closed questions is straightforward, as possible responses are implicit in the question. Coding is also usually uncomplicated, as respondents are confined to selecting a pre-determined response. Thus, as discussed in Chapter 4, it is important that the possible responses match the sentiments of respondents, otherwise the instrument will lack content validity. Missing data and poor reliability, which have to be addressed in the data processing and analyses, are a probable reflection and consequence of this. These issues should therefore be addressed early in the development and testing of the instruments (Chapter 4).

Multiple response questions, where respondents can select more than one response, or questions in which respondents are requested to rank responses according to their preference can complicate the coding procedures. In the development of the coding frame it is important to have a clear idea of the analyses that are required to fulfil study objectives; and to ensure that data are coded and entered into the database in such a way that allows the required statistical procedures to be performed. For example, if the researcher wished to compare first preferences of different groups of respondents, a variable relating to the first preferences would need to be separately coded and entered.

Missing values (codes) should also be designated for each variable (Field, 2005). When no data are entered for any question, it needs to be clear if this is because the respondent chose not respond to the question, the question was not applicable because of answers to other questions, an interviewer forgot to pose the question, etc. In some cases, responses may be ambiguous. For example, a respondent may tick more than one response when only one was required. Generally, this will have to be coded as missing, but there may sometimes be a case for creating a new code rather than excluding the case altogether. There may also be distinct patterns of missing data between the study sites, and this should be examined as it could lead to a systematic bias in the data.

Established instruments will have their own instructions for coding which must be followed by all. Instructions for coding, whether for established instruments or those developed by the team, must be clear to all members of the team, and included in the instructions for data

PERSONAL ACCOUNT 7.1

JAMES C MCELNAY

Pharmaceutical care research – working with European colleagues

---

Experience gained in leading two international studies relating to pharmaceutical care provision across Europe (Pharmaceutical Care Network Europe (PCNE), http://www.pcne.org/), one on pharmaceutical care provision to elderly patients (Bernsten *et al.*, 2001) and an ongoing study on the current stage of implementation of pharmaceutical care in community pharmacies (as a follow-up to previous work in Northern Ireland – Bell *et al.*, 1998), has provided some personal lessons relating to project management which are shared in this short summary.

Having formed the partnership, and having secured appropriate resources, it is important to have a launch business meeting where representatives from the different countries gather to agree the way forward. This will include detailed discussion on the protocol, roles to be undertaken by different contributors (e.g. statistical support), standard operating procedures for translation of questionnaires, target sample sizes, process control (i.e. to ensure the same procedures will be adhered to in all participating centres), time lines and the publication policy. This cannot be achieved unless the research leader carries the respect of the group and all group members are willing to compromise; for example if their preferred outcome measures are accepted for inclusion by the group.

If results are to be compared across countries, a uniform approach must be used. In more complex trials, this involves bringing together all the study materials and standard operating procedures into a project manual. Clear definitions are important, and in the early days, defining the term 'pharmaceutical care' itself, from a European perspective, created some interesting challenges. Ethical approval can also be challenging, especially relating to access to patient data, since privacy laws can differ in different countries. The major two challenges, however, relate to process control, i.e. making sure that, first, participating countries are progressing with the different stages of the project in unison and second, that what has been agreed by the group is actually being done. Pharmacist project diaries can be used to assist with this latter aspect; these must be carefully monitored.

Reporting of results to the co-ordinating centre must be carefully controlled. The best way to achieve this is for the co-ordinating centre to develop a common database which is distributed to all participating centres and for an agreement to be reached such that data will not be accepted unless presented in the agreed format. Agreement of a publication policy at an early stage is necessary, i.e. where and when individual country data can be presented as conference presentations, who will be the authors and when full papers on the work can be presented.

Such agreements and monitoring cannot be achieved without periodic face-to-face meetings, which need to be carefully minuted, with agreements and actions clearly stated.

Project management is common sense, you may say, but unless robustly put in place you can forget about having worthwhile results.

References

Bernsten C, Bjorkman I, Caramona M, Crealey G, Frokjaer B, Grundberger E, Gustafsson T, Henman M, Herborg H, Hughes C M, McElnay J C, Magner M, van Mil F, Schaeffer M, Silva S, Sondergaard B, Sturgess I, Tromp D, Vivero L, Winterstein A on behalf of the PEER Group (2001). Improving the well-being of elderly patients via community pharmacy-based provision of pharmaceutical care: a multi-centre study in seven European countries. *Drugs Aging* 18: 63–77.

Bell H, McElnay J C, Hughes C M, Woods A (1998). An assessment of pharmaceutical care by community pharmacists in Northern Ireland. *Am J Health Syst Pharm* 55: 2009–2013.

collection. In Personal account 7.1, which focuses on the importance of appropriate management structures and procedures in international studies, James McElnay highlights the value of a comprehensive 'project manual' which should include detailed instructions for coding.

In coding open questions, the codes will generally be based on the responses received. In an international study, responses to open questions are likely to be more diverse. The research team will have to agree categories of responses that they believe accurately reflect and distinguish the answers received, taking into account the additional complexity and potential context-specificity of international research.

Once a coding frame has been developed and agreed, the data can be coded. If the coding frame is well-matched to the data collection instrument and the data itself, then its reliable application should not be a problem. However, clear instructions regarding the operation of the coding frame should be prepared, in particular to ensure consistency in coding of any questions in which researchers have to exercise some judgement when coding a response. A common additional procedure is an assessment of inter-rater reliability. For this, a sample of questionnaires will be selected, independently coded by at least two researchers and the results compared. This may be particularly pertinent in international studies to be sure that coding frames are consistently applied across what may be diverse settings and by many researchers with variable expertise and experience.

The coded data are then generally entered into a database. A final process before the analysis commences is the 'cleaning' of the data. This refers to the process of checking the accuracy of the data entry process, identifying spurious values and correcting errors, which may stem from either the coding or the data entry processes. The value of a careful cleaning process cannot be underestimated. A single incorrect entry can invalidate a whole series of analyses and require these to be repeated. If, in an international study, coding of data and data entry are undertaken locally, procedures must be in place to ensure that these activities are carried out to a consistently high standard.

Diaries

Diaries are commonly employed to gather prospective data. Each participant (rather than an independent researcher) is responsible for maintaining their own diary and needs clear directions regarding what is to be included and the level of detail required (see Chapter 6). Participants in all locations and settings must share a common view of what is a relevant entry.

When it comes to the data processing and analysis of diary data, many of the principles and approaches discussed in relation to survey or interview data will apply. In terms of study design and data structure, the main difference is that data are prospective, relating to events over a period of time. This leads to some additional issues regarding the reliability and validity of the data which can be investigated, to some extent, in the processing and analysis.

When developing the coding frame in an international study, there may be important differences in the contextual or other factors surrounding the events being recorded which need to be reflected in the coding frame. For example, different patterns of healthcare provision or variation in types of pharmacy may be an important determinant of the frequency of events. If local factors, believed to be relevant, are excluded, this may affect the face validity of the analysis. Thus, it may be necessary to tailor instruments (see Chapter 4) and coding frames (e.g. by the addition of relevant variables) to local circumstances to ensure a full picture of the relevant factors surrounding events is obtained. The possibility of the impact of local factors should be explored in the preliminary fieldwork and pilot work as far as possible so that it can be integrated into the study design and objectives (see Chapter 2). However, care also needs to be taken to ensure that comparability of data between settings, regarding the events that are the subject of the study, is not compromised.

Quality assurance of the data should be guided by the potential threats to the reliability and validity. Relying on other people to collect data inevitably raises issues regarding their reliability. In diary research, concerns include recording fatigue: individuals may be diligent in maintaining their diary for a period of time, but this commitment may then wane. This will be reflected in otherwise unexplained decreasing numbers of entries. At busy times it could be difficult to maintain records and as a consequence some data may be lost. Conversely, when events are rare, participants may not remember that they are supposed to be making a record, or may forget the details that are to be included. Addressing these issues is important in the development of instruments (deciding the level of detail) and devising the data collection procedures (e.g. time period of data collection) to ensure data collection methods are acceptable and workable for participants in all locations.

Quantitative analytical procedures are commonly employed, particularly descriptive procedures. Following the development of a coding frame, data are coded and generally entered into a database for analysis. If local contextual factors are to be taken into account, independent analyses may be performed on local datasets in addition to the combined. Many of the procedures discussed in relation to survey research will be relevant. When diaries are used as a qualitative method, many of the principles and procedures discussed below, in the section on 'Qualitative analysis', will apply.

Observation

Observation enables data to be gathered concerning 'real life' occurrences rather than people's perceptions of events, and the specific issues concerning this type of approach has been discussed in Chapter 6. Here, we will specifically focus on processing and analysis of observational data, which can be either quantitative, qualitative, or include elements of both.

In terms of the reliability and validity of procedures some specific concerns arise in observational studies which, in an international study will be more complex to assess. The major concern in terms of the validity of data in observation studies is the 'Hawthorne effect' which describes the propensity for individuals to change their behaviour when they are being watched (see Chapter 6). The advantage of observation as a technique for gathering data on real life occurrences rather than people's recollections or perceptions of events (as in a survey) can be undermined by the Hawthorne effect. In devising the data collection procedures, researchers should attempt to minimise interference by being as unobtrusive as possible (see Chapter 6). However, it may be possible to make some assessment of the impact of the presence of the observer during the data processing and analysis. For example, some people compare data gathered at the start of an observation period with that collected at the end when people may have settled down into normal routines. Sometimes a limited amount of data can be collected by covert or other methods, enabling a comparison.

In an international study, the nature of the impact of the Hawthorne effect may vary between settings. For example, countries may differ in what is viewed as normal or acceptable practice. This may determine how individuals, when being observed, are likely to change their behaviours. In some locations, people may be more used to research and accepting of observers. There may also be differences in the extent to which people are confident about their practice and/or satisfied by assurances of confidentiality and anonymity of data.

Clear guidelines for observers in all settings should be prepared. Directions should relate to the identification of relevant situations or events about which they are collecting data, the features to be recorded and the level of detail. When a number of observers are involved, some comparisons can be made of data collected by each. This check on inter-observer reliability is achieved by ensuring a code identifying the observer is included in the coding frame and subsequently entered on the database. In an international study, similar checks can be performed. Complications may arise as a consequence of issues of validity as well as reliability. As for diary entries (see above) there may be background factors pertinent to particular countries/settings which are important to understanding the context of any event. In common with other international studies, coding frames and procedures should effectively reflect and enable interpretation of data in the context of local circumstances and perceptions. This has to be balanced against ensuring overall unity in the coding structures and procedures to enable analysis of the combined dataset.

Secondary analysis and existing databases

Existing datasets provide a useful source of data for some studies. In these studies the members of the research team themselves do not need to engage in any data collection. Their task is to identify relevant existing datasets and assess them for suitability against their study objectives. This will involve an appraisal of the content of the database (the variables included), the completeness of data and their reliability and validity.

The data may already be entered into a database, which may be in a suitable format for analysis to commence. In other situations the data may be maintained as either electronic records from which relevant information needs to be identified and extracted, or in the form of written records which need to be coded by the research team prior to any analysis. Not having to undertake data collection is generally a huge bonus in terms of the costs of a project. However, relying on datasets that have often been collected for another purpose can seriously limit their value in meeting a set of study objectives.

Thus, before analysis commences, a number of questions have to be examined by the research team: What data are included in the databases? Are the data of adequate quality in terms of completeness, reliability and validity? In an international study, where a common dataset may not be involved, the assessments have to be made separately for each, and an additional issue has to be examined: the comparability of datasets from the different locations. In terms of the content of the database, an assessment needs to be made of whether the database includes all the necessary information to enable the study objectives to be met. The absence of what is believed to be a key variable may render the database unsuitable for the study.

The research team will also have to make an assessment of the reliability and validity of the data. A first consideration may be regarding its completeness. If the database is not complete this will lead to questions regarding how representative it is of any population. An assessment needs to be made of whether the extent of missing data will unacceptably compromise the credibility of the study. Such an assessment may be possible if missing data are concentrated around particular variables which may be less important to the study objectives. However, if there is a suspicion that the database is incomplete in that whole cases may be missing, concerns may arise regarding the external validity, i.e. that the information may not be reflective of the study population as a whole. In some situations there may be little or no information regarding the maintenance of the dataset to enable the research team to assess its completeness in this respect.

In addition to its completeness, some assurances of the reliability and validity should be sought. The processes for this will depend on the information contained. However, for reliability some cross-checking and analyses to identify spurious entries may be performed and/or there may be an opportunity to assess consistency of information entered with paper records or between population sub-groups. In terms of the validity, an assessment will focus on the extent to which the data contained are likely to be a true reflection of the phenomena of interest. For example, can clinical or prescription data be accepted as a valid indication of diagnosis? Are drug-related problems adequately described?

In an international study, ensuring the comparability of datasets will raise an additional set of considerations. It is likely that datasets or sources in different countries will have been collected for differing purposes. They may therefore vary in the populations to whom they relate as well as the variables and measures included. The research team must be satisfied that all datasets meet the required standards in terms of the completeness, reliability and validity. Even if all datasets are judged as including the relevant information, it is possible that variables may have been measured, recorded and/or coded in different ways. For example, differing criteria may have been used to denote the severity of disease, varying levels of detail may be included regarding clinical outcomes, medication may be recorded by product name or class of medication. Sometimes some recoding of data will be possible and although this can be time-consuming it may enable a combined analysis. In other cases this may not be possible and a judgement will have to be made regarding the wisdom of combining information for analysis.

The analysis undertaken will depend on the study objectives. Descriptive or hypothesis testing procedures may be employed. In large datasets multivariate procedures may be appropriate, especially in an exploratory study where bivariate analyses would lead to a large number of tests, potential chance associations and difficulties in unravelling confounding between variables.

Quantitative analysis

The aim of this section is to provide an overview of statistical procedures commonly employed in quantitative studies, with a particular focus on data analysis and quality assurance in international studies. For a more detailed discussion of statistical theory and the selection and application of procedures to achieve specific study objectives, readers should turn to more specialised texts (Hamilton, 1996; Pett, 1997; Kirkwood and Sterne, 2003; Field, 2005; Munro, 2005; Scott and Mazhindu, 2005).

The structure of the data as normally distributed (or less commonly, corresponding to some other mathematical distribution) or non-parametric (distribution-free) is an important criterion in the selection of appropriate statistical tests. In addition, data relating to any variable will also be designated as nominal, ordinal or interval/ratio.

Descriptive procedures (especially frequency analyses and summary statistics) are employed in most studies. This is often the predominant approach in survey research. However, in experimental studies where the principal objective is to test a hypothesis, descriptive procedures will be used to provide information on sample characteristics and the study settings. Frequency analyses enable presentation of data in tables, bar charts, pie-charts, etc. Summary statistics (means, medians, measures of spread) provide a small number of parameters which are informative descriptors of the data. For normally distributed data, the mean and standard deviation (as a measure of spread) together provide a description of the dataset. For non-parametric data, e.g. data that are skewed, the median provides a more representative middle value of a dataset; interquartile ranges are commonly used as measures of spread.

Confidence intervals are employed to indicate the likely accuracy when generalising the findings from a sample to the wider population, and 95% confidence intervals are conventionally employed. For normally distributed data, the upper and lower values of the confidence interval are interpreted as the values between which the researcher can assume (with 95% certainty) the true population value lies.

Analytical procedures are also sometimes employed to compare population sub-groups, or in an experimental study to compare intervention and control groups. Again the choice of actual test will often depend on whether or not the data are normally distributed. To compare two groups, for which data are normally distributed, t-tests are often used; if there are more than two groups ANOVA may be applied. Non-parametric approaches to comparing groups are Wilcoxon or Mann–Whitney U-tests (two groups) and Kruskal–Wallis tests for more than two groups. For nominal variables, chi-square tests are commonly employed to compare counts between categories.

Tests of statistical significance are used to indicate whether or not differences between groups are likely to be chance occurrences (e.g. a result of sampling error) or a reflection of real differences between populations. Conventionally, a significance level of <0.05 is employed. A value below this indicates that the observed difference between the groups would have less that a 1 in 20 chance of occurring if there was no systematic difference between the groups. Thus, when a <0.05 criterion is applied, in 1 in 20 cases the researchers will draw an incorrect conclusion.

Multivariate procedures are employed in the analysis of large datasets when the inter-relationships between variables would be expected to be complex. Multivariate techniques operate by performing analysis on many variables simultaneously. There are a very wide range of procedures employed for different purposes and study objectives. Prior to their application, researchers must establish their suitability to the dataset and the study objectives. Common multivariate techniques include data reduction procedures (e.g. factor analysis, principal components analysis) in which a large number of variables is reduced to a smaller number by identifying those that are closely correlated. Multiple (and other) regression procedures aim to identify a series of 'independent' variables that are predictive of a variable of interest, which is designated the 'dependent' variable.

External validity: sample characteristics and response rates

In undertaking a quantitative analysis, the first stage is commonly to employ descriptive procedures to characterise the study sample and settings. In an international study this would generally extend to comparing participants between the different study locations. When data are available, researchers will also want to make some assessment of the extent to which participants are, and are not, representative of a wider population(s). Calculating response rates and comparing responders with non-responders is important in providing an indication of the likely representativeness of the sample to a population. This will enable an assessment of the potential response bias which will add greatly to the interpretation of the findings. For example, if all non-responders to a questionnaire survey about the use of pharmacy services were more likely to be older people, it would be important to take this into account before drawing any conclusions from the study.

In an international study, separate assessments of the response rates for each location should be made, as well as an examination of the profile of response bias. Recruitment to a study may be more successful in one centre than another which would have a differential impact on representativeness of the samples. These findings would be important in assessing the comparability of the samples and the external validity of the study (see also Chapters 4 and 5).

Descriptive procedures may also be applied to examine local features in the organisation of services, patterns of provision in the uptake of pharmaceutical care, use of medicines and any other social and cultural factors that may be important to the interpretation of the findings in one or more locations. These factors will also be important considerations regarding the advisability of specific analyses across the combined datasets.

Also important to the external validity is the potential sampling bias. In a study in which differing sampling procedures have been necessary in each site to accommodate local situations, this may be reflected in sample characteristics. Similarly if inclusion/exclusion criteria could be more effectively operationalised in some locations, the profile of the sample bias may vary between these locations (see Chapter 5).

Reliability and validity and the operation of research

Issues that may be examined to ensure the reliability and validity of the research process have been raised in the previous sections of this chapter in relation to the different study methods. In an international study, analysis focusing on the execution of research in different centres may be enlightening in terms of the likely quality of the data from each, and as a whole. Any differences in the operation of the research between sites, whether pre-planned or modifications to address problems once the study has commenced, should be carefully documented so that any potential impacts on the reliability or validity of data can be identified.

Decisions may need to be made regarding the combining of datasets from different locations or whether to exclude analyses relating to particular variables or cases. The data analysis may be designed to examine these concerns, and inform judgements regarding the validity of pursuing specific analyses. For example, assessments may be made of non-response profiles, patterns of missing data, and inter-rater reliability. In a study in which data are gathered by a number of researchers, some analysis is commonly conducted to examine consequent variation between them. In an international study, it may be expected that the execution of the research will be more successful in some locations than others. It is only when the research team is satisfied regarding the reliability and validity of the data, that analyses to meet each of the study objectives should be performed. In Personal account 7.2 Sabine Nebel and colleagues describe their experience of analysing data collected in six Mediterranean communities – and some of the challenges of quality assurance that arose.

PERSONAL ACCOUNT 7.2

SABINE NEBEL, MICHAEL HEINRICH AND FELICITY SMITH

Dietary patterns and consumption of locally grown foods in six Mediterranean communities in three countries

---

This study included a structured questionnaire to gather data from householders in six communities regarding socio-economic and other personal characteristics, health beliefs relating to the consumption of locally grown foods and dietary patterns. This was part of a wider study to identify health-conferring components of Mediterranean diets (Heinrich *et al.*, 2006).

The questionnaire included established and validated measures of health status (EuroQol-5D), the Food Frequency Questionnaire (FFQ), questions on sex, age, occupation, household structures, information on consumption of local produce and beliefs regarding potential benefits and risks to health.

Data were collected from householders in the six communities by different interviewers who were members of the research team. The structured instrument (questionnaire) was produced in discussion with, and including contributions from, members of the research team from each country, many of whom had differing views regarding the value and acceptability of different instruments in their local populations. However, agreement was achieved and the same questionnaire was employed in all locations in face-to-face interviews in respondents' own homes. A coding frame was prepared centrally, but this required discussion among team members in each site to ensure that it reflected differing patterns of consumption of locally grown foods in the contexts of lifestyles and diets of each of the communities. Data were coded by members of the research team in each country. As this involved individuals with varying levels of experience and expertise, it was important to ensure that everyone understood how the coding frame should be applied. On receiving the coded data from each interviewer, the consistency of the coding for all datasets was checked. An SPSS data file was constructed centrally and coded data from each of the study sites entered for analysis.

Data were coded so that cases from each country and community could be distinguished in the dataset. This enabled analyses relating to individual communities as well as the combined dataset. Analysis also included a comparison of response rates between the different communities. Descriptive procedures, especially frequency analyses and summary statistics, enabled the characterisation of the total sample across all regions as well as for each community. Cross-tabulations and non-parametric tests (Mann–Whitney and Kruskal–Wallis) were employed to compare sub-groups. Analysis of the full dataset provided an overview of the consumption of locally grown foods in the context of population characteristics and lifestyles across the Mediterranean communities and regions. More detailed analyses relating to each country or community could be performed by the researchers who had been involved in the collection of these data, and had insights into the pertinence and value of different aspects of the study in the context of local issues and perspectives.

Reference

Heinrich M, Müller W, Galli C (guest eds) (2006). *Local Mediterranean Food Plants and Nutraceuticals. Forum of Nutrition 59.* Basel: Karger.

Qualitative analysis

The approach to data processing and analysis in qualitative research, whilst differing greatly from that of quantitative studies, presents a number of similar challenges in international studies. The conceptual approach to qualitative research: theoretical frameworks, purposive sampling, in-depth interviews following principles of qualitative enquiry, is followed by analytical procedures to illuminate phenomena in the context of the settings in which they occur and thus to provide insights into how and why different situations or behaviours arise and/or bear certain features (Miles and Huberman, 1994; Berg, 2004; Bryman, 2004; Green and Thorogood, 2004). Thus, it will immediately be apparent that an international study may be expected to present a more diverse range of environmental, organisational and socio-cultural factors that provides important contexts for the interpretation of the data. A valid approach to data processing and analysis must enable an assessment of the phenomena of interest in these contexts. Indeed, in an international study an important objective of the research is often to identify similarities and differences between locations and attempt to explain these through a more detailed analysis of each dataset and wider organisational or socio-cultural or other features that are characteristic of each location.

Verbatim transcription of all interview or focus group data is generally the first task in data processing. Verbatim records are considered a necessity for ensuring that interpretation of responses remains an accurate reflection of the perceptions or experiences presented by respondents. Unlike many single country studies, in an international study the issue of language and the potential need for translation may arise. The data from each location could be treated as an independent dataset, analysed in situ, in the local languages, and reported as separate outputs. If this approach is taken, a method of combining results and feeding them into the international project needs to be devised. This could be achieved by agreeing an analysis framework and then providing a pro-forma report, which could be produced on the basis of one – or a few – 'pilot' focus groups, as is described in Personal account 6.1 of Ellen Schafheutle and Karen Hassell (page 107). This approach would then need to be followed by all country partners, who would produce separate country reports. These would ideally be all in the same common language, follow an agreed structure, and contain sufficient detail, to allow cross-country analysis and interpretation based on just the reports. If a number of different languages are involved this will mean that only quotes included in the report will need to be translated and cross-checked for cultural meaning and translational equivalence (see Chapter 4).

However, if the datasets are to be combined prior to analysis, translation of data could lead to concerns regarding the validity, i.e. accurate representation of sentiments expressed (see Chapter 4). It will also have major cost and time implications, as all data will require translation (and back-translation), where long passages of interview transcripts, for example, may not be pertinent to the study objectives. A judgement will need to be made on which approach should be taken, but it is likely that resources will not allow translation of entire qualitative datasets.

The development of the coding frame generally commences with the derivation of a primary coding structure. The researchers must have gained sufficient familiarity with the data (often achieved through data collection, transcription and/or reading of transcripts) to identify broad themes that arise. These themes are then given labels which become primary codes. In true qualitative work, the primary codes should 'emerge' from the data, (cf. a grounded approach) rather than being pre-conceived. In an international study, the range of perspectives raised and discussed may be diverse, reflecting differing social and cultural constructs from which they emanate. It is possible that a common coding structure does not provide an accurate reflection of phenomena in all settings. If this is seen as a potential problem, it may be advisable to develop a coding frame for each dataset independently and compare them prior to making any decision regarding the application of a common coding frame. Potential questions regarding the objectivity in these processes can also arise in that individual researchers will inevitably hold their own perceptions which could colour their interpretation of the data. The usual practice in single-centre studies is for at least two researchers to independently devise coding structures, which are then compared. In an international study, similar procedures across national boundaries could be employed to ensure objectivity.

Once (one or more) primary coding structures have been devised, the data are coded, i.e. sections of the transcripts relevant to each theme are identified and labelled as such. Reliability is generally checked by having more than one person coding the data and the results of this being compared. As long as adequate care is taken, discrepancies between coders often reflect a lack of clarity in the coding frame which can then be remedied. However, in an international study the application of codes may be more problematic as, as a consequence of greater diversity in responses, it may be less clear whether a particular viewpoint or comment falls within any category. Thus, reliability in coding procedures should be checked for each setting to ensure that all data relevant to any particular theme are consistently recognised and labelled as such.

Following the application of primary codes, more detailed secondary coding structures are commonly developed. These follow similar principles and procedures to the derivation of primary codes, but they are intended to enable a more detailed analysis of the primary themes. Thus, the coding structure may allow a more detailed description of events, identify associated factors, attempt to examine the circumstances in which particular situations arise, or look for explanatory clues regarding people's beliefs and behaviours. Once again, in an international study to maintain validity it will be important to ensure that coding structures enable an accurate and relevant classification of data from each setting. It may be that a coding frame which provides an effective framework for these questions in one location is unsuitable in another. Decisions will have to be made regarding the validity of a common coding frame, modification that may be required in different locations or whether development of coding frames for each location should proceed independently. Frances Owusu-Daaku and Felicity Smith (Personal account 7.3) describe the application of these techniques to qualitative interviews with Ghanaian women resident in Ghana and the UK.

Qualitative research is sometimes viewed as possessing an inherent validity because the conception and design and execution of the study is focused on examining and explaining events and/or behaviours in relation to real life situations. However, as a sole argument this is generally inadequate. In qualitative research, a number of approaches can be employed to address concerns about the validity of the research.

PERSONAL ACCOUNT 7.3

FRANCES OWUSU-DAAKU AND FELICITY SMITH

Comparing health beliefs and behaviours in two independent samples of Ghanaian women: coding, analysis and interpretation

---

The aim of the study was to compare the health beliefs, health-seeking behaviours and use of medicines in two independent samples of Ghanaian women: resident in Kumasi, Ghana and London, UK (Owusu-Daaku and Smith, 2005). Interview guides were prepared for each group. While the principal themes were common to both samples, to achieve the objectives of the study and reflect the differing contexts regarding the provision and delivery of healthcare, some differences between the schedules was necessary.

Both interview guides asked about actions taken with regard to illnesses, perceptions and beliefs about causes, experiences and use of health services and use of medicines or other remedies. These themes provided the basis for the primary coding frame which was applied to both sets of interviews. That is, responses relating to these themes were located in each of the interviews and coded.

From this point forward the two sets of interviews were processed independently. This was necessary to ensure that secondary or more detailed coding within each of these themes reflected the responses of the two groups. For example, in terms of health behaviours and use of services, respondents would discuss their actions in terms of the availability and organisation of different types of care which are known to differ significantly between the two locations. Thus, in developing the coding frame these differing contextual factors and consequent health behaviours had to be separately identified and examined for the two samples. Furthermore, some topic areas were relevant only in one location, e.g. experience of Ghanaian women of services provided in the UK.

At the end of the interviews some personal information was gathered on the respondents. Quantitative descriptive procedures were used to characterise the participants in each of the samples, which were drawn from two populations of differing social settings, structures and outlooks. For example, respondents in both samples were asked about their employment status. While the responses to this question may be valid in the context of each sample, employment structures and measures may not be comparable between the two. For example, designation into formal categories of employed/unemployed may have different realities between the two settings. Information on the number of years of full-time education was also gathered. Variation between the two samples on this variable may be viewed as a valid indication of differing social status of the two groups (i.e. a potential confounding variable).

Thus, it was only following the data analysis that comparisons of the two datasets were undertaken, i.e. the findings rather than the data were compared. Comparing the findings highlighted both similarities and differences in health beliefs and use of medicines by the two groups of women. It enabled some conclusions to be drawn regarding Ghanaian women's perceptions of the extent to which they differ from indigenous British women in health beliefs, behaviours and use of medicines as well as ways in which they adapt to a new setting.

Reference

Owusu-Daaku F T K and Smith F J (2005). Health-seeking behaviour: perspectives of Ghanaian women in London and Kumasi. *Int J Pharm Pract* 13: 71–76.

Adherence to principles of qualitative enquiry is vital if the results are to possess any credibility within the research community or among peer-groups and stakeholders. Some quality assurance is important. This applies to all stages of the work, from the conceptual framework of the research, selecting an appropriate design, a skilled approach to interviewing, as well as techniques during and following the analysis of data (see Chapters 4, 5 and 6).

To promote validity, by examining phenomena in greater detail in their natural settings, an iterative approach to data collection and/or analysis is sometimes taken. For example, subsequent phases of data collection may be designed to enable further examination of preliminary findings in one or more locations. Sometimes the study is designed with this in mind. That is, some analysis is performed following an initial collection of data, and the findings of this inform the next stage of the data collection.

Another approach involves the re-examination of data in an attempt to refute preliminary findings (i.e. identify data that are inconsistent with a hypothesis). This involves revisiting the data to look for any instances that are inconsistent with the study conclusions and therefore suggest that these may not be correct. In an international study, this investigation could be extended to data from each location, to check the applicability of findings to each. That is, the extent to which findings apply in separate datasets could be independently assessed. This could involve an attempt to generate competing descriptions and/or explanations from the datasets of different locations.

Conclusion

In international studies many considerations arise in the data processing and analysis as a consequence of the need to combine independently collected datasets. Ensuring that study objectives and procedures are relevant to, and workable in, all settings pervades decision-making at all stages, through the conception, management and conduct of the study. Data processing and analysis give rise to their own issues regarding maintaining the scientific validity of the work as well as providing an opportunity to address issues of quality assurance that stem from methodological approaches and experiences in the execution of the research.

References

Berg B L (2004). *Qualitative Research Methods for the Social Sciences*, 5th edn. London: Pearson.

Bryman A (2004). *Social Research Methods*, 2nd edn. Oxford: Oxford University Press.

Field A (2005). *Discovering Statistics Using SPSS for Windows*, 2nd edn. London: Sage.

Green J, Thorogood N (2004). *Qualitative Methods for Health Research*. London: Sage.

Hamilton L C (1996). *Data Analysis for Social Scientists*. Belmont, CA: Duxbury Press.

Kirkwood B, Sterne J (2003). *Essential Medical Statistics*. Oxford: Blackwell Science.

Miles M B, Huberman A M (1994). *Qualitative Data Analysis*. London: Sage.

Munro B H (ed.) (2005). *Statistical Methods for Health Care Research*, 5th edn. Philadelphia: Lippincott, Williams and Wilkins.

Pett M A (1997). *Nonparametric Statistics for Health Care Research: Statistics for Small Samples and Unusual Distributions*. London: Sage.

Scott I, Mazhindu D (2005). *Statistics for Health Care Professionals*. London: Sage.

8

Dissemination, project conclusion and final thoughts

This, the final chapter serves two purposes: it discusses the final stages of an international project, which usually culminates in the dissemination of its findings, and it concludes this book. It thus aims to provide a summary of the issues and challenges that have been discussed in the course of this text, from setting up and clarification of aims and objectives, through instrument design and data collection, processing, analysis and interpretation. It will begin by focusing on the challenges of publishing from an international project.

Dissemination and publication in international projects

Key to any researcher's agenda is the interest, need and responsibility to publish the research findings to appropriate audiences. This is likely to result in numerous different types of (possible) publications, many of which will be based on the reporting of findings (both positive and negative). Furthermore, some will focus on the project findings' implications for policy and practice, and there may also be opportunity for sharing insights into particular methodological issues or challenges, especially at an international level. There will be scope for analysis and publication at national level, specifically drawing out findings and implications for any of the participant countries. International publications (especially in peer-reviewed academic journals) are likely to report comparisons across countries and are the ultimate goal for international collaborations.

The different types of publication will aim to satisfy the requirements of national and international academic audiences, but they will also ensure that issues of national and international importance are shared with the relevant stakeholders at different levels and in an appropriate format. Besides, there is likely to be some variation in the agendas of individual researchers, who will have their own personal and professional aspirations, a need to satisfy institutional expectations, as well as desires to share the findings of the research. Differences in the importance of such academic, institutional and personal agendas could lead to conflicts among team members throughout the project, but especially at the publication stage, if these have not been explicitly agreed at the beginning of the project. An early goal for the international research team should thus be to set up and agree a dissemination strategy that meets the needs of all members of the team and addresses the goals of the research. This can be revisited as the project gets underway and develops, as certain elements and their relevance for publications may become clearer. All agreements regarding ownership of datasets, access to, and use of, the data, including independent analyses of national or combined datasets that could lead to publication, should be well documented and justified.

When drawing up a publication strategy, issues that ought to be considered therefore are: what to publish, who the relevant audiences are and why, what type of output would suit each audience (e.g. written/oral report, publication in a peer-reviewed journal, conference communications, presentation at professional/key meetings), in which languages and when to publish. Basic expectations and working agreements will need to be established. This will include clarification on lead and co-authorship, as there may be culture-specific views of authorship and publication that need to be discussed (Delamont et al., 1997). However, publication and dissemination of the findings is the culmination of the research process. This should be a collective undertaking and an integral component of any research endeavour.

All team members may need to give thought to, and take responsibility for, the co-ordination of reporting in a broader context and their duty to ensure both positive and negative evidence is disseminated. Differences in the practices of publication and the associated expectations between academic disciplines and cultures may compound certain difficulties, including local traditions and practical constraints. Concerns about the political implications of the research findings may have a high focus for certain members of the team, e.g. how the findings may reflect on individual members of the team, how others (external to the research team) may use the research findings to the potential detriment of individual team members, or the impact of research findings on the future development of services in particular settings. It cannot be assumed that the agendas of individual team members concord with the goals or outcomes of the research. Furthermore, funding bodies and other significant individuals who may have been part of the approval process in order for the research to take place may have their own perspectives about the publication of findings.

From setting up to publishing – a summary of the elements of international research

Before, once again, emphasising the importance of good project management and effective communication, we would like to summarise the process of an international project, and the pertinent messages associated with each stage. In her personal account, Marion Schaefer illustrates some of the issues that may arise during the course of an international collaboration (Personal account 8.1).

PERSONAL ACCOUNT 8.1

MARION SCHAEFFER

Improving the well-being of elderly patients via community pharmacy based provision of pharmaceutical care – a multi-centre study in seven European countries

To plan and conduct international multi-centre studies usually requires an already well-established network of researchers who are equally motivated to strive for new scientific outcomes. Therefore, it is helpful when at least some of them know each other from annual scientific workshops or conferences, which makes it easier to choose the study centre which has the main responsibility for the application process and the compiling of the final report.

The study design has to be thoroughly discussed right from the beginning to identify all possible structural and functional differences in the participating countries. The group should spend some time explaining to each other – as an example – the course of a structured care programme and the framework in which it is embedded, for example special incentives set by the sickness funds or insurance companies.

In a second step it has to be checked whether all requested primary data can be collected in the same way in each country: For instance when the dose of a medicine is required and there is no obligation in some countries to note the dose on the prescription one has to find other ways of requesting it, by asking the patient directly for example. The forms used for documentation must be applicable in each participating country.

During the study it is important that the members of the international study group meet regularly face-to-face to discuss problems arising in their

continued overleaf

Personal account 8.1 (continued)

countries and to make sure that all national study centres proceed with their work in the same way and keep the time schedule. In addition, all participating pharmacists must receive the same training programme after they have been enrolled into the study. The PEER group met twice a year in one of the seven member countries. As the Elderly Study was supported by the European BIOMED Programme, financial resources for these meetings were provided (Bernsten *et al.*, 2001).

For the final analysis of data the study centre has to build up a database into which all national data can be incorporated. Therefore, it is recommended that the research group co-operates with a statistician from the very beginning of the study.

Discussion of the results usually requires a dual approach, focusing first on the pooled data and second on the variation of results from different countries. An interpretation of these differences is often difficult when there is insufficient information about the healthcare system in each country. One example of inconsistent results from the Elderly Study were differences in the health-related quality of life: in most participating countries the patients' health-related quality of life remained the same or declined, but in Denmark significant improvements were seen in some SF-36 domains for intervention patients while there was a decline in the controls.

An economic evaluation of structured care programmes has to consider detailed information about national healthcare programmes and especially reimbursement regulations. The traditional relationship between pharmacists and GPs also may have an influence on the outcomes.

In general it is recommended to follow a streamlined approach to data collection for a limited number of research questions to avoid assessment overload for patients as well as pharmacists.

Reference

Bernsten C, Bjorkman I, Caramona M, Crealey G, Frokjaer B, Grundberger E, Gustafsson T, Henman M, Herborg H, Hughes C M, McElnay J C, Magner M, van Mil F, Schaeffer M, Silva S, Sondergaard B, Sturgess I, Tromp D, Vivero L, Winterstein A on behalf of the PEER Group (2001). Improving the well-being of elderly patients via community pharmacy-based provision of pharmaceutical care: a multi-centre study in seven European countries. *Drugs Aging* 18: 63–77.

The importance for international research of good and effective early planning was emphasised in Chapter 2. This may involve literature reviews in the different national contexts, where some relevant publications may not be available in English. Insight into the different countries' traditions and, in particular, healthcare systems, allows the formation of valid and meaningful aims and objectives across the participating countries. Part of this is accessible through the literature, but the value of speaking to people who live and work in the different locations should not be underestimated. Valuable resources in this respect are, first, the actual project team members, but also the thoughts of an advisory group and reflections of stakeholders which may be examined as part of the preliminary work. Any insights gained will need to be shared adequately with the project team members, so that all achieve a common view of the objectives and contexts of the research. This will usually involve some face-to-face contact.

In Chapter 3 important universal ethical principles and their application in international research were discussed. While rules and regulations may differ between countries, all requirements must be met. Processes can be time-consuming, but observance of high ethical standards and ethical review will be a priority to international researchers, and an important part of the preparatory work. Good communication between team members regarding the requirements of different countries and a co-ordinated approach to meet these should be in place.

Instrument development and validation was the topic of Chapter 4. We discussed the importance of designing instruments that are meaningful and valid in all countries. Instruments will often need to be applied in more than one language. The importance of suitable processes of translation and back-translation, to ensure equivalence in language, interpretation and meaning in the context of culture, was highlighted as a challenge in the development of instruments for international research. Chapter 5 addressed issues of sampling and recruitment of participants, and the potential difficulties of ensuring comparable populations and samples, identifying recruitment strategies workable across settings, while observing the principles of sampling theory. Chapter 6 set out some more practical aspects of actual data collection using different approaches. These included questionnaire surveys, qualitative interviews or focus groups, observation, diaries and documentary research; triangulation, and why this may be particularly relevant in international studies, was also discussed. Again, the emphasis was on ensuring that data collection using any method is done in a way that will ensure the production of valid and comparable data in all partner countries. Chapter 7 demonstrated how, even at the later project stages, international research poses challenges. In particular, combining (commonly independent) datasets from different countries requires special attention to ensure that during the analysis and interpretation, the scientific integrity is assessed, demonstrated and maintained. Much groundwork will have been done when designing instruments and agreeing on response categories, and possibly designing a codebook or coding frame to be used by all. Nevertheless, combining datasets for analysis will require both care and also a high level of trust amongst all team members, regarding adherence to protocols and standards of data collection processes. This will be supported by an agreement between all as to how to use and analyse the data, and ultimately disseminate the findings.

Project management and communication

As good project management with clear channels conducive to effective communication are so crucially important to all stages of an international project and its ultimate success, their main elements will be reiterated to conclude this book. Any research project presents a number of challenges that need to be identified and discussed, and agreement needs to be reached on how to address and resolve these. If a project involves a number of partners and teams, particularly if they are part of an international collaboration, these challenges tend to be more complex and will be associated with greater risks. Team members are located in different institutions and countries and often speak different languages. Due to the multidisciplinary nature of research in health and medicines, researchers can have varying professional backgrounds and thus paradigms, which affect their perspectives on, and approaches to, the project's aims and objectives. These different disciplines may also possess their own conventions around, and use of, language, terminology and meaning, even if all speak English. Therefore, a common understanding of the same words or terminology cannot necessarily be assumed.

Indeed, effective communication is a key to successful international research where cultural, linguistic, economic and other barriers may prevail between researchers (Benatar, 2002). However, the remoteness of the different team members presents a barrier to the opportunities and means to achieve good and regular communication. Today's technology allows us to communicate while in different locations, using e-mail and tele- (or video-) conference facilities, which are invaluable means for exchanges on progress. Nevertheless, face-to-face meetings are absolutely essential for a successful international collaboration. This is exemplified in Personal account 8.2 by Claire Anderson, which further describes the importance of good and trusting relationships among team members.

PERSONAL ACCOUNT 8.2

CLAIRE ANDERSON

Working on international research projects

I have worked on a number of international collaborations. One of the most important factors in developing successful projects has been building strong relationships. Then when you wish to work together you know each other well enough to communicate effectively via e-mail or telephone. You may also already have papers together which may strengthen any bid to a research funder. However, I believe that this is no real substitute for making time for face-to-face meetings where relationships can be made much stronger. Moreover, this will enable collaborators to begin to understand each other's cultural values, discuss any politics involved and to explore differences in health systems, university systems and priorities. It will also allow time to understand each other's strengths and weaknesses, ensuring more effective utilisation of combined skills.

One successful application has been with a South African colleague plus two British colleagues, one of whom had moved to the UK from the South African colleague's institution. The rest of us had known each other well for over ten years. I had visited South Africa three times. When we came to write the application we were able to work effectively using e-mail communication and further refined our project when three of us met at a conference.

Another application which was highly rated but unsuccessful was with an Indian colleague. I had built a relationship with her over a number of years and had given two seminars at her pharmacy school. We had also already written a joint paper. I was fortunate to receive a grant from my university to go to India to write the bid with my colleague in Bangalore. We were able to spend two days sitting writing the grant which saved a lot of time and meant that we both had ownership of it. We were not successful this time and I later found that only those applications that had a UK Indian on board got funded in the call for bids because the British Council were concerned about the difficulty of navigating the bureaucracy of the Indian higher education system.

A further example is a recent success in securing two University of Nottingham and Government of Malaysia-funded PhD scholarships for university lecturers in Malaysia. The students are required to spend a total of one year at Nottingham but do their fieldwork in Malaysia with a second supervisor at their own university. An ex-PhD student of mine had recently returned to the lecturer's university; as an academic she was keen to develop her research so will act as their supervisor. Again this is based on strong existing relationships developed over a number of years.

continued overleaf

Personal account 8.2 (continued)

I have also been involved in a number of European projects with multiple project partners. Again face-to-face meetings where there has been time for social interaction proved invaluable for building relationships, understanding each other's priorities and discussing cultural, political and bureaucratic issues.

While face-to-face meetings during an international collaboration are essential, they are costly and so the team requires explicit goals for the effective running of team meetings so that they remain part of the motivating strategy of collaborative working. Ground rules to optimise team working, e.g. compulsory attendance, an agreement to complete any preparatory work in advance of the meeting, collaborative problem-solving, sharing of resources and/or information, honesty about progress, identifying the need for support, may all be factors that ought to be considered. The format of meetings may also be pre-designed according to the priorities of the research at that given time, for example: prompt starts, goal setting, procedures for resolving serious difficulties and making records of progress. Due consideration needs to be afforded to local and individual factors, including cultural working practices among team members.

Good project management will be essential for effective team meetings in particular, but also effective working throughout the project. Team members not only need to agree upon the goals of the project and their roles and responsibilities, but also to act accordingly. An appropriate management structure should encompass and foster good communication, but also provide a framework against which progress is maintained and assessed. In any collaboration there is likely to be a certain hierarchical structure, with one project lead. This will usually be the lead applicant on any joint funding application and thus the partner who holds overall responsibility for the project. This does not, however, mean, that this partner will necessarily lead on all aspects of the project, but will often delegate according to the specific expertise and capacity of others. In EU (BIOMED) funded projects, such action is usually referred to as 'reinforced action', whereas the activities that all partners are involved in to similar extents are termed 'concerted action'. (This stems from the idea that members are playing different instruments in a concert, where each player contributes towards the piece of music that is being performed. The conductor would equate to the project lead.)

Which partner(s) take(s) on what role for which part of the project needs to be clear to all team members through all stages of the research. If one partner assumes the lead on one particular aspect (reinforced action), the precise expectations of other partners and the timing of this needs to be agreed and clear ahead of time, so that all team members can plan their workload accordingly. Any unmet requirements or deadlines are likely to jeopardise timely progress, which is essential in order to reach the final project goal and outcome at the agreed date.

Conclusion

While this chapter concludes the book, the topics discussed are not intended solely as final thoughts but are issues that should be revisited and addressed throughout the entire collaborative process. An essential component to effective team working is appropriate management and good communication and this is important through all stages of any project, yet presents particular challenges in international collaborations.

In the personal accounts included in this book, many of the challenges of international research were highlighted. However, despite any difficulties, the contributors were all positive regarding the opportunities that involvement in an international study affords. We hope that this book will encourage others to participate in international projects; and that the discussions and advice in the text, along with the reflections in the personal accounts, will be an aid to successful collaborations.

References

Benatar S R (2002). Reflections and recommendations on research ethics in developing countries. *Soc Sci Med* 54: 1131–1141.

Delamont S, Atkinson P, Parry O (1997). *Supervising the PhD: A Guide to Success.* Buckingham: The Society for Research into Higher Education and Open University Press.

Further reading

Anderson S (ed.) (2004). *Managing Pharmaceuticals in International Health*. Basel, Boston, Berlin: BirkHauser Verlag.

Babbie E (2007). *The Practice of Social Research*, 11th edn. Belmont, CA: Thomson Wadsworth.

Behling O, Law K S (2000). *Translating Questionnaires and Other Research Instruments*. London: Sage.

Berg B L (2004). *Qualitative Research Methods for the Social Sciences*, 5th edn. London: Pearson.

Black N, Gruen R (2005). *Understanding Health Services*. Maidenhead: Open University Press.

Bowling A (2002). *Research Methods in Health* (2nd edn). Buckingham: Open University Press.

Bowling A, Ebrahim S (2005). *Handbook of Health Research Methods*. Maidenhead: Open University Press.

Bryman A (2004). *Social Research Methods*, 2nd edn. Oxford: Oxford University Press.

Bryman A, Cramer D (1997). *Quantitative Data Analysis with SPSS for Windows: a Guide for Social Scientists*. London: Routledge.

Cresswell J W (2003). *Research Design: Qualitative, Quantitative and Mixed Methods Approaches*. London: Sage.

Field A (2005). *Discovering Statistics Using SPSS for Windows*, 2nd edn. London: Sage.

Foster C (2001). *The Ethics of Medical Research on Humans*. Cambridge: Cambridge University Press.

Green J, Thorogood N (2004). *Qualitative Methods for Health Research*. London: Sage.

Hamilton L C (1996). *Data Analysis for Social Scientists*. Belmont, CA: Duxbury Press.

Hanson E C (2006). *Successful Quantitative Health Research*. Maidenhead: Open University Press.

International Pharmaceutical Federation: www.fip.org (accessed 19 December 2007).

Kirkwood B, Sterne J (2003). *Essential Medical Statistics*. Oxford: Blackwell Sciences.

Koop C E, Pearson C E, Schwarz M R (eds) (2002). *Critical Issues in Global Health*. San Francisco: Jossey-Bass.

Lavery J V, Grady C, Wahl E, Emanuel E J (2007). *Ethical Issues in International Biomedical Research*. Oxford: Oxford University Press.

Miles M B, Huberman A M (1994). *Qualitative Data Analysis*. London: Sage.

Millennium Development Goals website: www.un.org/millenniumgoals (accessed 19 December 2007).

Munro B H (ed.) (2005). *Statistical Methods for Health Care Research*, 5th edn. Philadelphia: Lippincott, Williams and Wilkins.

Oppenheim A N (1992). *Questionnaire Design, Interviewing and Attitude Measurement*. London and New York: Pinter.

Pawson R, Tilley N (2004). *Realistic Evaluation*. London: Sage.

Payer L (1996). *Medicine and Culture*. New York: Owl Books.

Pett M A (1997). *Nonparametric Statistics for Health Care Research: Statistics for Small Samples and Unusual Distributions*. London: Sage.

Robson C (2002). *Real World Research: a Resource for Social Scientists and Practitioner Researchers*, 2nd edn. Oxford: Blackwell.

Scott I, Mazhindu D (2005). *Statistics for Health Care Professionals*. London: Sage.

Skolni K (2008). *Essentials of Global Health Research*. Sudbury, MA: James and Bartlett.

Smith F J (2002). *Research Methods in Pharmacy Practice*. London: Pharmaceutical Press.

Smith F J (2005). *Conducting your Pharmacy Practice Research Project*. London: Pharmaceutical Press.

UN Millennium Project (2005). *Prescription for Healthy Development: Increasing Access to Medicines*. London: Earthscan.

World Bank (2004). *The Millennium Development Goals for Health*. Washington: IBRD.

World Health Organization website: www.who.int (accessed 19 December 2007).

World Health Organization (2004). *The World Medicines Situation*. Geneva: WHO.

World Health Organization (2006). *Working Together for Health: The World Health Report 2006*. Geneva: WHO.

Index